This is my life story, which I started writing in 2014 or so. Once I began, the memories came flooding back – some of them joyous, others heartbreaking. My husband, John, was staggered by my recall of my early childhood and youth.

I have tried to be honest throughout, while maintaining confidentiality where other people are concerned. John always urged me not to 'cover up' where we had failed each other and the Lord. The only things I have concealed, occasionally, are the real names of a few of the people we encountered.

I dedicate this book to my three children, Mary, Matthew and Ana. You are so much a part of my story and I love what you have contributed to it, and the great sense of humour we shared as a family.

I dedicate it also to the memory of my soulmate, the great adventurer John Hart. Together we faced armed robberies, cockroaches and snakes, and confronted our own failings and limitations, while living a life in which belief proved to be transformative and full of grace.

Finally, I want to acknowledge Jill Knox, who helped me to organise my writing, and Huw Spanner, who edited it with meticulous skill. I am grateful to them both for their kindness and good humour.

Brenda Hart

My Life
So Far...

Brenda Hart

Dear Lucy,

With much love,

from Maurice.

✗

And Me! Brenda ✗

First published in 2023 by Queen of Harts Publishing

ISBN 978-1-3999-5752-6

Printed in Great Britain by IngramSpark

Cover design: Jules Richards

Foreword

This is a remarkable book, full of humour, pain, adventure and dedicated service to God. Members of the family will relish reliving all the amazing experiences that they went through together. Close friends of Brenda and her late husband, John, will read it praising God for his remarkable faithfulness to them, in the way he protected and provided for them, often in extreme circumstances. Readers who never met this committed Christian couple will find themselves drawn into the story and may find it difficult to put the book down, even though there is much detail at times to work through.

The opening chapters tell of Brenda's childhood, during which she lost her mother and was bed-ridden with tuberculosis. The story continues with her nursing career, her commitment to God and her response to an invitation at the Keswick Convention to serve her Lord wherever he might call her. Unknown to her, the young man she would later marry had had a similar call to give his life in service to God – in the same country.

The rest of the book records the amazing ministry they had together, first in Ecuador and then back in England. It is compelling reading. Brenda's memoirs conclude with the death of her much-loved husband as a result of vascular dementia.

I have known both John and Brenda for over 50 years and can vouch for their integrity. I was with them through the many challenges they faced. I often felt deeply for them and agonised in prayer during their struggles, as well as rejoicing with them as their work in Ecuador developed.

My wife and I loved our visit to their home in Santo Domingo de los Colorados, where we witnessed first-hand the churches they had planted and the Orphaids centre they established to cater for mothers who were dying with Aids with their children around them. It became obvious to us during our stay just how much they loved the people they were caring for and how much they were respected and loved by those they were working with.

If you take the time to read this book, you will be inspired and challenged by the price that Brenda and John were willing to pay in serving our wonderful Lord. The apostle Paul urged his protégé Timothy to 'endure hardship as a good soldier of Jesus Christ ' (2 Timothy 2.3, NKJV). This wonderful couple certainly took their share of hard knocks in their ministry, from sickness to armed robbery. How often most of us are tempted to give up when confronted with difficulties!

You will be inspired and challenged, too, by their willingness to depend totally on God for money, especially when they sailed to Ecuador with a young family. The way that God protected and provided for them is a wonderful example of his care for his children. Their faith in their heavenly Father shines through the book.

Finally, I believe you will be inspired and challenged by Brenda's candour in sharing the pain they went through when their marriage was under pressure. It stemmed from John at times putting his ministry before his family, which resulted in first Brenda and then their children feeling dreadfully neglected. There is an important lesson in this for everyone involved in Christian ministry to get their priorities right: God first, family next and then our work for him.

Brenda and John have created a wonderful legacy of Christian faith and commitment which their children and grandchildren have embraced. When you have finished the book, consider taking a few moments to kneel and make a fresh offering of your own life to God.

Victor Jack

Chapter 1

I suppose I should begin by saying something about my parents. My father, William, was the eldest child of William Hughes and Martha Ball. He had two younger sisters, Lilian and Gladys. My mother, Alice, was the eldest child of William Lee and Harriet (or 'Hettie') Kent. She had a sister, Hester, who died from tuberculosis of the lungs at the age of 16, and a much younger brother, Harold. He was a real favourite of mine.

My parents were distantly related and had known each other in childhood. They married in 1935, when my father was 21 and my mother 19. I was born on the 9th August 1937 and was followed 15 months later by my sister, Marlene. I was five when my brother, Maurice, arrived in 1943. The day my mother was taken to hospital to give birth to him was the last time I would ever see her.

I have one very vivid and precious memory which must be from late 1942. It is very dark outside and there are heavy curtains drawn across the windows because of the wartime blackout. We are sitting together in the light of a crackling fire and Marlene and I are helping Mammy and Dad as they make a rug out of old material. I recall an atmosphere of security, love and happiness as Dad told us funny stories.

That memory was to come back to me many times over the years after my mother died. Sometimes it comforted me, sometimes it filled me with sadness and a deep longing for what I had lost; but as I grew up it gave me a goal and a hope.

I have a vivid memory of my final separation from my mother. There was an air raid that night and I remember the siren going as we rushed to the shelter. Dad picked me up and Mammy was somewhere behind us with little Marlene, who was crying loudly. There was a lot of confusion and people running. Dad carried me down into the shelter and then went back to help Mammy. He was about to set Marlene down next to me when Mammy cried out as she missed a step and fell.

By now, we could hear the frightening thud of the bombs. I went to Mammy and she folded me in her arms. She was rather shaken up and seemed to be in a lot of pain – she was crying more and more. When eventually the raid was over and we emerged, she had to be lifted out. I heard one of our neighbours say to my dad, 'I'll get Alice to hospital, Bill. You take care of your babies.'

I remember clinging to her, overcome with fear that I would never see her again, and screaming: 'Don't take my mammy away!'

Maurice was born with tuberculous glands, and my mother was diagnosed with systemic TB. When she was brought home, to our terraced house in the village of Cutsyke, Marlene and I had already been sent to foster parents, 10 miles away in Leeds, so that Dad could take care of her undisturbed.

I don't recall the name of the lady who looked after us, but she was plump and jolly and very affectionate, and my sister and I were very well cared for. My memory is rather hazy, but I do remember the hurt of not seeing my parents and not understanding why we were separated.

After a month or so, they realised that I had got TB, too, and I was taken to a sanatorium in the Yorkshire Dales. It seemed to happen very quickly and I have no recollection of anyone explaining to me what was going on or why. I had to have a lot of very nasty medicine, and injections – which I dreaded! It was all very frightening.

I had my sixth birthday there and the nurses and the other children in the ward all sang to me. They tried to make me happy, but it seemed only to increase my pain. The deep sense of loss was dreadful. In time, I did make friends, though, and generally I think I coped well. I have some very clear memories, and most of them are happy.

There was a kind and cheerful girl there called Jean who was a few years older than me. Everyone seemed to love her and I soon grew very fond of her. I would tell her my deepest secrets and she always seemed to know when I was miserable and would give me a hug.

Jean was in the sanatorium because her knee was infected with TB, which caused her a huge amount of pain, especially at night. One day, she was told she would have to have her leg amputated, which distressed her greatly. I tried in my childish way to comfort her, but for a while she was inconsolable.

The awful day came and she had the operation. She was given lots of attention by the nurses and doctors, as well as some amazing gifts from her family. I remember longing to be Jean – but later, when I witnessed her pain and her sense of loss, young as I was I realised that it was better to have two legs than all the presents in the world!

As the months went by, we were allowed out of bed to go and play. Eventually, we were well enough to be moved to a different part of the sanatorium, where there were little boys, too. One of them, who was called Donald, was about my age and he was such fun, he made us laugh a lot. Sometimes he would mimic the nurses; occasionally he would go too far and get into trouble for being rude or disobedient.

One day, he and I got into a really frightening scrape. We were playing on a large area of grass in front of our veranda when Donald said to me: 'Do you see those trees? They're the edge of a big wood. Let's go and explore!'

So we did – and we got ourselves hopelessly lost. At first, it seemed like a great adventure, but as time went by and the daylight began to fade we both became afraid. It grew quite dark and we huddled together at the base of a big tree and started to cry. Eventually, we heard people shouting and saw a bright light, and one of the nursing sisters came into view. When she found us, she was cross and glad at the same time.

We were taken to see Matron, who made us stand in a corner with our faces to the wall. It was at this point that a huge sob burst from me and I cried for my mammy. Matron called me to her and sat me on her knee and held me close. Then she called Donald over, too, and put her arm around him. We were forgiven.

We promised that we would never do such a thing again. Donald took great delight in telling the other children about our adventure, but he never admitted that my crying for my mother had softened Matron's heart!

Jean was soon to be going home and childishly I resented that and felt angry with her. When she finally went, I was broken-hearted. It seems to me that I was very unhappy for a long time. What upset me even more is that I started to wet the bed – a problem that persisted for some years.

The only unkindness I can recall at the sanatorium was when I was suffering badly from conjunctivitis. One of the night nurses thought I was making it worse by rubbing my eyes and, to stop me, she tied my hands to the frame of the bed. What a wretched night I had! Someone must have told the other nurses, because it never happened again.

Not long after, Donald was told that he would soon be going home as he wasn't infectious any more. I was pleased for him, but also deeply upset. I did have other friends at the sanatorium but that time stands out in my memory as very bleak. I felt a deep, dark loneliness, as if I had been abandoned.

We used to sleep on the veranda in the summer and I remember one night when I lay awake, crying and longing for comfort. After a while, worn out by my misery, I looked up at the night sky and was suddenly overwhelmed by awe at its vastness. The moon was very bright, as I recall, and there were thousands of twinkling stars, and yet the sky looked like black velvet.

Who made the world?, I wondered. Who made the sky,

so far away and so beautiful? Who made me? Why was I here? Why was I sick and alone? Strangely, I knew deep down that there was a Creator, so I told him how I felt and asked him to take care of me. I felt comforted and eventually fell into a deep and peaceful sleep.

This childhood memory has stayed with me all my life. I now believe that God heard a very unhappy little girl's cry for help, and has cared for me and watched over me ever since.

It was only a few months before I was discharged from the sanatorium that I learnt that my little brother was also there. Maurice was now three and had been there from about three months old. His TB had affected his ear and he had had to have quite a bit of surgery before he could come to the sanatorium.

The first time I met him, I was overcome with emotion. He was a beautiful, blond little fellow, who looked like an angel – and I loved him instantly. He was my brother and he needed me (I was yet to learn just how difficult that could be). I played with him, trying to get to know him, but he was like quicksilver, very unpredictable, and full of uncontrolled energy.

A day came when Maurice and I were discharged from the sanatorium. We had both been there three years. Dad came to collect us – oh, the excitement of it! I was happy, but also a little frightened, though I didn't know why. In fact, this huge change for Maurice and me was to prove traumatic for all of us.

On the long journey home, I sat next to my dad and we were both rather quiet at first, being somewhat nervous. We had travelled a fair distance when he asked me shyly if I was glad to be going home. Truthfully, I said I was but I was also a bit sad to be leaving the friends I had made. I was also afraid that Marlene might not remember me, and might not like me.

Eventually we arrived at Castleford, the nearest town

to our village. My Aunty Gladys was waiting there with my sister and she caught me up and gave me a wonderful hug. Then she brought Marlene forward and said: 'You two make friends while I talk to your dad and get to know Maurice.'

She had arranged to have a photograph taken of the three of us, which is actually the only picture there is of any of us as children. It was a week before my ninth birthday; Marlene was seven-and-a-half and Maurice was three.

Chapter 2

This part of my story is really painful to write. Going home had been my constant dream, but the reality was at first unlike anything I had remembered or imagined. Everything seemed so drab and dirty. The village was surrounded by 'muck stacks', mountains of spoil from the nearby pit at Glasshoughton, and there was no grass or trees. Our house, in the middle of a long terrace, was tiny, cold and dark, with very little furniture.

The initial excitement of being with my family started to ebb away. Dad looked rather sad as he said, with forced brightness, 'We'll soon have a nice fire and some hot soup. It's been a long day!' He was so patient with Maurice and me, and Marlene tried to be friendly – but nothing that first day seemed right and later, in bed, after my sister was asleep, I cried and cried with disappointment. In part I was crying for my poor dad, who was having such trouble to please us and make us happy.

The next day began badly: I had wet the bed. My shame was awful – and, to add to the humiliation, Marlene would not stop going on about it. As we shared the bed, I could see her point of view! This was to make all our lives difficult for many years – Maurice, too, was a bed-wetter – and caused quite a lot of tension, misunderstanding and misery.

Our house had four rooms. Downstairs there was a sitting room, with a settee, two armchairs and a sideboard with cupboards and drawers. This was known as 'the front of the house' and you entered it by the door from the street. Behind it was the kitchen, a smaller room with a table against one wall and a 'range' against the opposite wall, a shiny black affair with an oven and a huge fire-guard in front of it.

On the back wall was a large, deep sink under the

window and, next to it, a 'set pot' for boiling clothes (when you had lit a fire under it). A door led out to a back yard of hard-packed earth, with a path leading to an outside toilet.

Both rooms had a cement-tiled floor part-hidden under a homemade rug made out of old clothes. There was little light, but they were clean and snug and, as young as I was, I could see that Dad had tried to make everything look its best.

Upstairs was very cold and rather stark. One bedroom contained a double bed and a wardrobe. The floorboards were bare, like the stairs, and the bedding seemed to be a mix of blankets and coats – it didn't look very inviting at all. The other room was smaller and even more drab, with a much smaller window letting in little natural light. There were two single beds in this room, including a very small one for Maurice.

There was no bathroom. We washed our hands and faces in the kitchen sink every morning and had a 'strip wash' at the end of each day. There was a tin bath hanging up outside in the yard which was brought in to the kitchen every Friday evening for our weekly bath. I would go first, then Marlene, then Maurice, with Dad topping up the hot water after each of us had got out. He would have his bath once we had gone to bed.

As I look back, I realise that although our home was a great disappointment at first, it became very precious to me. So much of the influence of my amazing dad and my memories of him as I grew up are tied up inextricably in that house.

Marlene hadn't remembered me and had never met her brother before. I think it was all very frightening for her when we came home, and she became very possessive of Dad. Both Maurice and I had huge insecurities and at first our life together as a family was very strained. My sister and I fought a lot, and our little brother was so out of control that at times things became quite manic. Dad told us that, nonetheless, whatever happened, we had to forgive and look out for each other.

In September, Marlene went back to school. I had hoped to go, too, but the mothers of the local children were afraid I was still infected with TB and they got up a petition to stop me. I was heartbroken! I had missed so much schooling already – we had not had a teacher in the sanatorium because of the war – and I so wanted to learn to read.

So, instead, I looked after Maurice while Dad was at work. At nine years old, I was the carer of a very disturbed little boy of three.

Every morning, Dad would strip Maurice's bed while I stripped mine and then I would rinse out the soiled bedclothes. After breakfast, once Dad had gone to work and Marlene to school, I would attempt to wash and dress my reluctant little brother. He was a squirming bundle of arms and legs and often would run away from me.

Sometimes I would see the funny side of the situation and become almost hysterical with laughter, but at other times I got frustrated, and even angry. To this day, I have feelings of guilt about my dealings with Maurice!

The first couple of years back home saw times of real struggle and hardship, and yet my lasting memories are of fun and warm, fuzzy feelings towards all our friends and neighbours.

Just opposite our back yard lived one of my dad's second cousins, who was known to us as Aunty Lena. She was married to a gentle man called Ben and they had three children: Gary, who was almost 11, Alvin, who was a bit younger than me, and Lana, who was about seven. They were all so good to us! Aunty Lena was always helpful, the children were great playmates and we were always made welcome at their house. The children would come over to our house, too, and we felt like one family –

they were 'our Gary', 'our Alvin' and 'our Lana'.

Six doors away from us lived an aunt and uncle of Dad's, called Blanche and Tommy. They hadn't been able to have any children of their own, but not long after Maurice and I came home they adopted a baby girl, who they named Norma.

They, too, were so kind and patient with us children! We were always made welcome at their house and often they would give us some little treat. We were very taken with the new baby, and when she was a little older we loved to take her out in her pram and play with her.

There were some real characters in our street and Marlene and I would fall about laughing at the names Dad gave them. One lady, Mrs C, who often came by, would fold her arms over her ample tummy and ask Dad: 'Have you done your ironing?' (or some other chore). Dad told us that from now on she was to be known as Mrs HYD.

After that, whenever she stopped by to chat, we children would nudge each other and giggle as we waited for her to start asking 'Have you done...?' Dad would look at us and wink and set us off laughing again. One day, she told Dad he had the happiest children in the street – 'always laughing, they are!'

One youngish man my dad made friends with had been badly affected by the war. He was always turned out immaculately in his soldier's uniform, his hair neatly cut and his shoes well polished, and he would march around with a stick under his arm. His hard-pressed wife had a houseful of children and so we kids would help her. She always referred to her husband as 'my poor Joe', so that's what Dad used to call him. The whole community really cared for him and his family.

One amazing lady who will always stay in my memory was Mrs Dunnington. I think she had lost her husband in the war and she didn't have any children. Her house was diagonally opposite the back of ours and she could see into our kitchen window. On many a dark evening, while Dad was still at work, she would notice us sitting in the firelight because the money had run out in the gas meter and she would come over and call outside the back door, 'Are you dear bairns in need of gas money?'

Of course we would say yes, and she would come in and put a penny in the meter. It was all done in such a businesslike way and then out she would go with an emphatic 'Goodnight, dear bairns!'

Mrs Dunnington kept ducks and chickens and we would take vegetable peelings and stale bread round to her house for them, and sometimes we'd help her to clean up the back yard where they lived. We were always 'dear' to her, and Dad was 'dear Mr Hughes'. His name for her was 'dear Ducky'. He was so grateful for her watchful eye on us! She often gave us little treats but she was never intrusive in her kindness.

There were a few people in our community who we regarded as 'posh'. They were in the retail trade and had bigger homes, in a neighbourhood slightly apart from the rest of us. Among them, Mr and Mrs Hartley and their daughter, Barbara, were quite special to us. Barbara was two years older or so than me and she seemed so refined, always nicely dressed – and she didn't speak in our flat-vowelled Northern dialect. She went to a different school from us and wasn't able to play with us much. Many of the other local children would mock her and be unkind, but we felt sorry for her.

Mrs Hartley was always giving us clothes, for which we were very thankful. On one occasion, she found out that Marlene and I were in a play at school and she came round to our house to say that she wanted to help us with our costumes. What fun she made of it all – and when we performed the play, she and her husband and Barbara came to cheer us.

Best of all were our immediate neighbours. On one side of

us were 'Uncle' Bob and 'Aunty' Ivy and their son, Cecil. He was four years older than me and had just started at the boys' grammar school when I came home. He was very polite but seemed to be shy and rather nervous – he never played with the rest of the children in the street. We thought it was because he had such a lot of homework but Dad thought that him being an only child made his parents over-protective.

Uncle Bob and Aunty Ivy would watch over the three of us when Dad was at work, especially during the school holidays. If we had a plan to do anything, we would tell Aunty and if she said, 'I don't see that's a good idea,' we listened – most of the time! We did get into some scrapes, but she would never tell tales to Dad. Many a cut or bruise she dealt with when things ended in tears, followed by a kiss and a cuddle.

On the other side of our house lived an amazing old lady called Mrs Wallbank. She was a widow but she had lots of grown-up children and grandchildren. She never complained about anything and always saw the bright side of life, even though she had gone through a lot of sorrow herself – she had lost several sons in the war, and another in a pit accident.

For all her optimism, though, she was never glib or dismissive about other people's struggles and hurts. When my mother was dying, and anguished at the thought of us and Dad being without her, Mrs W had been her comforter, encouraging her to trust in the heavenly Father and to pray for us all every day while she was still alive. Some years later, Mrs W told me that my mammy had found real peace with God and had entrusted each one of us to his care. Dad would share his troubles with this dear lady and found her a true confidant.

It was through Mrs W that we got to go to Sunday school. She had told Dad that he would have a few hours of peace while we learnt about the Bible. She was to play a larger role in my story as I grew up, but I will leave her here for now.

In our two streets, at the front and back of our house, we had quite a number of friends and we did a lot together. Whenever we could, come rain or shine, we would be outdoors having fun. We used to have skipping contests, for example, and invented all sorts of difficult jumps. We played with whipping tops – we would make a pretty pattern on a top with coloured chalk and when it span it would look quite beautiful. Then there was a hopscotch craze (the boys didn't like this much, though, and often made trouble, which led to a bit of pushing and pulling and shouting).

There were also a lot of ball games – some that we played together and some we played on our own. We also had conkers and jacks; and we would walk around on tin can 'stilts', holding on to bits of string to keep the cans under our feet.

Often we would all go off for a day, laden with huge sandwiches and homemade ginger beer or dandelion-and-burdock. We would enact something out of history, like a battle, or play Robin Hood and his Merry Men. Our imagination was never lacking – I don't remember ever being bored!

Of course, we all had domestic work to do for our parents, and Marlene and I more than most as we didn't have a mother and were responsible for Maurice as well.

Also, Dad decided that I could earn some money doing chores for some of the neighbours. The first one I did was for Mrs W: every Saturday morning, I would go and clean the toilet in her yard and, after that, her kitchen floor and all the work-tops. When all was done, I would sit with a cup of cocoa and a biscuit and she would get the Bible and read some special passage to me and explain what it meant. Then she would ask me how I was and listen to what I said with kind attention.

Going to work for Mrs W was something I treasured. She told me many things about my mother, and she always gave me sixpence and an apple or orange and lots of love. When she died suddenly, when I was about 12, it was an awful shock and the whole neighbourhood was in mourning. I and my family had lost someone very special – really, she was the grandmother we needed.

We did have actual grandmothers, of course. Dad's mother lived two bus rides away, so we hardly ever saw her; and she died not long after Mrs W. She was quite stout, and fresh-skinned and rosy with thick white hair, like a granny in a picture book. We knew her as Granny Brownridge, as she had remarried after our grandfather's death.

I remember one bright but very cold autumn day during the school holidays when we children decided to go and visit her. We set off really early and walked all the way to her house – she was amazed to see us! She soon had us warming ourselves by the fire with mounds of bread and dripping (melted fat from roast meat) and lovely hot, milky drinks.

When it was time to go, she came to the bus stop with us and I have the fondest memory of her standing there, a heavy shawl around her, her white hair blowing in the icy wind, waving us goodbye.

Our other grandmother had also been a young widow who had remarried. Granny Howarth lived about 15 minutes' walk away. She was very thin and seemed rather sad. She had suffered a lot: not only had my mother died young but she had lost an even younger daughter to TB – and I think she had made a bad choice for her second husband. If Grandad was out when we called round we were always made welcome, but if he was in she would talk to us outside and ask us to come some other time. She died when I was about 13 years old.

On occasions, Dad would take us to the cinema. I couldn't cope with Westerns or any film that involved any violence or threat – I don't know why, but I would start to feel panicky if ever I saw a person or an animal in danger. So, instead we usually went to see a musical, all singing and dancing, with Doris Day or Fred Astaire. I think even Dad liked those films, because we could all learn the songs and that made us happy.

We could all hold a tune well. I had a clear, strong soprano voice and Dad had a lovely tenor and could really sing – he was very musical. Many an evening we would just sing together and Dad would get out his mouth organ and take us down memory lane. In the holidays, the local cinema held a singing contest and Dad always entered his three children, and he was so proud when, more often than not, we each came first in our year group.

We would busy ourselves for days organising concerts in our yard, involving all the kids in the neighbourhood, and then we would invite all the mums and dads to come and hear us. Such a lot of happy memories!

Of course, there are bad memories, too. Things could be hard in the winter. I would get painful chilblains on my hands and feet. The house was so cold in the morning that the water would be frozen. When we got back from school I would try to light a fire, but my hands were numb with cold and I would get cross with Marlene and Maurice.

I started school for the first time when I was 11. I was thrust straight into secondary school and at first I was lost, but I had a fantastic teacher who helped me way beyond the call of duty. She gave me extra reading lessons on Saturdays, and told me many times a week that I was a clever little girl and once I began to read I would soon catch up. I was determined to learn.

Once I was able to read, I became a real bookworm. What a joy it was to hide away from everyone and read till

I was nearly cross-eyed! My appetite for books made me
a bit strange and set me at odds with Dad, Marlene and
Maurice and many of my friends.

For me, school was the happiest place to be, I was
learning so much and the teachers were so encouraging.
My memory of school is of four years of being excited
with learning. I worked very hard, but I had such fun,
too – the playground was a hive of activity. Just before
playtime we were given a half-pint bottle of milk each. I
loved milk but some of the other kids didn't, so I would
beg their bottles, too, and often I had a pint and a half!

Even so, despite all that milk – and all the second
helpings I would get from the smiling school dinner ladies
– I was a skinny little thing. I didn't start to develop until
I was 16 or so, and even when I began working I still
looked like a child.

I have one memory of learning something that I didn't
like, about myself.

One day, I got held up at the end of school and so the
friends I used to walk home with went on without me. I
started out to catch them up, but just outside the school
gates I saw something shiny on the ground and I stopped
to pick it up. It was a gold ring, with three jewels: a
diamond in the middle, with a sapphire on either side. I
was entranced by its beauty – for some reason, jewellery
always fascinated me – and so I decided to keep it.

That ring made me so wretched! I would bring it out
and admire it secretly, but then I would reflect that
someone must be very sad to have lost it – but then I
would tell myself: 'I haven't stolen it and it's really mine
now.' This went on for two or three days, until I realised
that to be happy again I would have to do the right thing
and hand it in.

Of course, it would be difficult to explain why I had
taken so long, but in the end I plucked up the courage
and, with shame written all over my face, I went to one

of the teachers and told her the whole story, not without
a few tears!

She was very kind and told me I had learnt an
important lesson: that to have self-respect we have to be
honest, no matter what it costs. She also explained that
if I didn't listen to my conscience and obey it, there was
a downward slope that could lead me to other, worse
behaviour. After those days of struggle, the relief was
wonderful. As the teacher said, I had regained my self-
respect.

When I came to the end of my time in secondary school,
I was offered the opportunity to continue my studies;
but Dad said it was impossible for me to stay in full-time
education. This caused me such disappointment and
sadness! I so wanted to go on learning – I had developed
a deep desire to be a nurse.

Chapter 3

Dad had worked down the mine from a very young age, like his Welsh father before him, and as a result he suffered from silicosis. He was taken ill when I was 13 or so, though I think it had been some years coming on. He had been working loading and unloading timber for some company, but when that became too hard for him he got a less arduous job at the glassworks, which he liked better. But soon he could not do that, either, as even walking left him breathless and he became very thin.

The very nice nurse who had helped when Maurice and I left the sanatorium came to see him often. She had beautiful red hair, so my dad called her 'Nurse Ginger', and of course we called her that, too. One day, she confided in me that Dad was very ill and needed an operation called a 'lobectomy' to remove the lower part of his left lung. He might have to spend six months in hospital and we children might have to be put in care – something that Dad was determined would not happen. Naturally, this was all very frightening for us!

In the end, I went to live with his sister, Aunty Lily, Marlene went to stay with his aunt, a very kind old lady who we knew as 'Aunty Ethel', and Maurice went to Aunty Lena, my dad's second cousin who lived opposite our back yard.

My time with Aunty Lily was not a happy one. I felt that I was a burden to the family. Donald, my cousin, was about two years older than me and was rather cold towards me. He treated me as an inferior and when he had friends round they all took pleasure in teasing me and making fun of me. I used to go to my room and weep at the humiliation.

Aunty Lily, too, was very distant towards me. She found fault with the way I spoke and the way I ate, and often made me feel worthless without actually saying anything. I found it all deeply distressing. Naturally, I was very concerned for my dad but he was never spoken of in that house as far as I can recall. I felt that my aunt did not have much love for him or for us children.

One redeeming feature of that period was that my aunt had another son, a little four-year-old called David. He and I were great pals. I found consolation in entertaining him and making him laugh, and I read to him, too, which he loved. When I finally went home, after six months or so, it was little David who cried and begged me not to go and told me he would miss me.

I never visited my aunt and her family afterwards, and I lost touch with that part of my family.

It was fantastic to be home again and reunited, though sadly my dad never got any better and was never able to do a proper job again. The health visitor came fairly often and on one occasion she told me that he was a very sick man and that we children must look out for him as much as we could.

Dad soon got himself a little work in the community, mending shoes in our back kitchen. It certainly helped to supplement his 'national assistance' and keep us fed and clothed. I had been thrilled to go back to my school – I don't recall going to school while I was staying at my aunt's – but that, too, came to an end and just before my 15th birthday I started work at the Town Tailors, a clothing factory 20 minutes' walk from our house. I did an eight-hour day and earned 30 shillings a week.

When I started, I was taking out tacking stitches, which was the most boring work imaginable. Some of the school-leavers I shared a table with were really rough-and-ready types and I found them quite intimidating.

However, our supervisor, Hilda, was a gentle, softly-spoken woman. She was much older than us and was badly disabled by rheumatoid arthritis, but what an influence for good she was to all us girls! I could see that she didn't like us using bad language or being unkind to each other, and in her quiet way she taught us some manners. She made quite an impression on me then, and was to have a profound influence on my life. (She would turn out to be a favourite aunt of my future husband!)

I had a very happy social life – my sister and I used to love to dress up on a Friday night and go dancing. I had friends from the Brethren church, but after I left school I kind of drifted away from church a bit. Whenever I passed the building, I would feel a pang of discomfort if I had not been for a while.

One evening in 1952, coming home from work at 5.30, I was passing the church and was surprised to hear singing. Dad told me that a Scottish evangelist had come to preach and the neighbours said he was very good, so I decided to go to the next meeting. I found it not just interesting but somehow exciting – the speaker, a man in his late thirties whose name was Adam Chambers, certainly knew how to hold one's attention!

His theme was the life and person of Jesus. I was captivated and went to all the following meetings, seized by a desire to know more. I had gone to church and Sunday school for years and had always loved the Bible and its many and varied stories. Dear Mrs W had read the scriptures to me and had told me many things about the Lord; but Mr Chambers' preaching was so powerful, I really felt that God was talking to me personally.

I realised that Jesus was God. I had kind of known this already in my head, but somehow this was a revelation that gripped me and moved me deep, deep down in my very soul. I needed to respond, and so in one of the meetings, quietly in my seat, with tears I surrendered to Jesus. It was an amazing sensation: I can only say that I felt a liberation, a coming home, as an indescribable love flooded my being. This experience set the course of my life thereafter.

One of the elders, an old man called Mr Ritson, lived next door but one to us and was like a grandfather to me. I was such a tyke in those days that when I told him I'd come to know the Lord, he said: 'Well, we'll see, won't we, Brenda!'

In fact, that 'all things new' sensation was to remain with me for a very long time. I was enchanted by Jesus, and drove my family and friends mad with what they saw as an obsession. I made many more friends at church and started going to meetings in a nearby town called Featherstone, where I met the most amazing family. Mr and Mrs Fryer had five children: Audrey, the eldest, who was a teacher; David and Mary, who were about my own age; Margaret, who was a little younger, and Philip, who was younger still.

Mrs Fryer was so motherly to me and my presence in their home was not only accepted but encouraged. The whole family treated me with great kindness and taught me so many good and wholesome lessons, but Mary and (much later) Philip were the best friends I could have had.

Since the age of 15, I had been going through a difficult time emotionally. I had become prone to moods and sometimes I felt so frustrated and angry and confused inside that I became very stroppy at home, slamming doors and stamping my feet. My lovely, poor dad hadn't a clue how to deal with me! I look back now with horror at the way I treated him at times. Being a Christian and behaving as I did, I suffered terribly from feelings of guilt and shame and remorse.

I confided in Mrs Fryer and, very helpfully, she told me that this was a normal but painful process. 'Brenda,' she explained, 'you have grown up without a mother and that is very hard. The Lord is kind and patient with his children and he knows just how mixed up you are feeling. Keep talking to him about everything, and keep repenting and saying sorry.' What a wise lady she was! She also gave me some instruction in the facts of life – I was a complete innocent.

From 1954, I became more and more bored and unhappy at the factory. For some time I had been studying in the evenings at the local college of further education and I had become a cadet nurse. I so wanted to be a fully qualified nurse, but I did not have enough education to get into the training required. It was very disappointing.

I really needed to have a heart-to-heart with Dad about how awful my job was – but the housing people were moving us to a new location and so nothing could be decided anyway until we had settled in there. What an amazing change that was! Some aspects of it were very positive, others very difficult. We were moving three miles away, to Airedale, a brand new estate of three-bedroomed, semi-detached houses that had been built largely to relieve the overcrowding in London, where so many buildings had been destroyed by bombs in the war.

Our new home was number 32 Hobart Road. The front door led into a small hall, with the stairs on the right. Straight ahead was a door into a very large room, which was a sitting room-cum-dining room, the latter part at the far end which led into a good-sized kitchen. Upstairs there were two large bedrooms and one very small one, plus a very nice bathroom. Like all the other houses, there was a small front garden and a very large garden at the back.

Our immediate neighbours were Yorkshire people. Mr Lamb was a miner, employed in the local pit, and Mrs Lamb was a housewife with a large family. Two of their youngest children, Walter and Mary, were the same ages as me and Marlene and we became good friends. Mary comes back into my story much later.

Almost all the other people on our street were from the East End of London. How different they were! Some were different in a nice way; others were rough and always seemed to be having noisy family arguments. A number of the women were beaten by their husbands, which really distressed us, and Dad, Marlene and I were forever rescuing some unfortunate victim!

One poor woman had not long since given birth when her husband came home drunk and started to hit her. She managed to run outside with her baby and we took her in for safety. Someone had called the police, which was just as well because her husband came round to our house and was trying to get in.

Sadly, this sort of thing happened far too often. We had a lovely new house, but we had lost all our friends and our community. At least the Lambs next door were really nice.

I now had to go to work at the factory by bus. The work was all so repetitive that even though I was now a machine operator I was very unhappy there.

Maurice was almost 11 and had to go to a different school, which he found very hard. He was very small and thin and was pushed around a bit, I think.

After we had been in the house for four months or so, the health visitor came to see us all. She was concerned mainly to see Dad, who was coping with his emphysema and managing to keep house. Marlene, who was now working at the same factory as me, was fine and so was I; but she was very worried about Maurice, who was still very small. (Some time later, he was sent to an 'open air' school in Grassington, North Yorkshire.)

The health visitor asked me how I was and so I told her: 'I'm well, but I'm very unhappy about the work I'm doing. It's so boring!' I added that I would love to study more – she knew I was going to night school – and that I wanted to become a nurse. 'Don't give up on your dream, Brenda!', she said.

She arranged for me to see a careers adviser in the town, who told me to look into some form of caring. I was given the name of a Dr Barnardo's children's home in Ripon and I applied and was invited for an interview. I was very impressed with the home and I felt that my interview had gone well. When I asked whether there would be any chance that I could continue to study in the nearest college, I was assured that something could be arranged.

Not long after, I received a letter telling me that I had a job, helping initially with the small children. How excited I was, and so were Dad and Marlene!

I started work at the home a little while before my 17th birthday. It took me a few weeks to settle in, as I felt shy at first. I loved the work, though, which was a great help. To begin with, I was put in the play room, with another girl called Rosie who was a bit older than me. Our job was to care for the little ones, from about two to four years old, and to play with them, mainly in groups.

The mornings flew by. After lunch, the little ones had a sleep and then if the weather was fine Rosie and I took them outside, or if it was raining we went back in the play room with them. Slowly I learnt to change nappies and comfort these dear little children and got to know them and their little ways. They all loved cuddles.

Most of the staff were people from the area, practical and down to earth. I don't remember any bad feeling – it was a happy place to be.

The nearest church was a big Methodist church and when I was free I would go to services and other meetings there. Some of the nurses went there, too. There was a good-sized youth group and naturally I became a part of it, and loved it. A young married couple called Jimmy and Anne ran the group and they soon started to include me in all its activities.

One important thing I was taught at that church was that it was important that your friends should know right from the start that you were a Christian, and if you got the chance you should tell them how you had come to know the Lord as your Saviour. We all got a bit of training in how to give our testimony.

At this time, I was growing as a Christian, my work in the home was getting better and better, I was learning all the time and being given more and more responsibilities. I also managed to get back to studying, one evening a week plus some homework. Life was exciting!

After I had been at Ripon for 18 months or so, the matron had a visit from someone who turned out to be director of the Mission of Hope, which ran a place in Croydon for unmarried mothers. (It seemed that this was the way these poor girls were dealt with, because their families didn't want the shame of it all.) Matron told her about me and we were introduced and it was decided that I would go to work for her, helping first with the babies and then eventually with the midwifery. The lady's name was Adeline Wallis.

I was to have another adventure!

Chapter 4

For the first six months in Croydon, I was to be given just a place to sleep and all my meals – I had to approach my churches to see whether they could provide me with some spending money. Both the one in Cutsyke and the one in Ripon helped me in this way.

Once again, I had quite a change to face, but life was great, mostly. Some of the other workers gave me a bit of a hard time to start with – they didn't like my Yorkshire accent – but things got better after a while. Eventually, I was put on the delivery unit, where my job was to assist the midwives, just doing whatever they asked me to do; but my! how stimulating it was!

After the six months, I was called in to see Miss Wallis. 'Brenda,' she said to me, 'you are an intelligent young woman and a natural nurse. I think you should go home to Castleford and see if you can get into nursing by the back door, as it were. I shall give you a reference, so you must mention me in your application and take it from there. If this is what the Lord wants for you, it will happen and you will know you are going in the direction the Lord wants you to.'

I followed her advice and I was given an interview. They then said they would get back to me when they had seen my references. A few weeks later, they contacted me again to invite me for a second interview – this one to take all day!

My family were as excited about all this as I was, and so was everyone at church. All my Christian friends were praying. What a mixture of excitement and nerves I felt! This was something that only the Lord could do for me, so I committed the whole thing into his hands. 'Whatever happens,' I prayed, 'please help me to cope, with success or disappointment.'

When I arrived, I was given a cup of tea and a biscuit

and then I was called in to see Matron. She told me: 'We are hoping you will be successful – you have very good references – but because you don't have all the academic qualifications we look for, you have to sit an intelligence test. After that, you will be given lunch, and later you will see the board of governors and they will ask you some questions.'

Wow! I was so keyed up I trembled when I walked into the room where the governors were waiting.

What a nice group of men and women they were! They soon put me at my ease. It wasn't like an interview at all, they just chatted with me and even had me laughing at one point.

After I left the room, I was given another cup of tea and told to wait. In a while, one of the lady governors came to find me with Matron, who shook my hand and said: 'Congratulations, you've been successful. You'll hear from us very soon to tell you what happens next.'

I didn't have to wait much more than a week for their letter. I was to be in the March 1957 intake of the large 'preliminary training school' in Harrogate, where all the hospitals in West Yorkshire sent their student nurses. I was given a list of study books I had to buy along with lots of paper, notepads, different-coloured pens and so forth. I would spend three months in PTS.

How fantastic it was to see Harrogate again! I was able to look up some of the friends I had made while working in Ripon. However, the time I spent in PTS was very intense. Most of the other students had all the advantage of having gone to grammar school and got some O-levels, and I realised from the start that I would have to work harder, and perhaps study longer, than anyone else. But it was fun, too. The lecturers were good to me and if ever I couldn't understand something I would see them afterwards – if I didn't have to rush to another lecture.

Opposite the buildings where we student nurses lived, there was a police cadet college. The student nurses saw the cadets and socialised with them quite a lot, going to dances and generally having fun. However, I knew that I had to work hard and not play. It was so very important for me to pass the final exams at PTS; if I didn't, I would lose my place and that would be the end.

There was also my Christian stand – young people then were heavily into drinking and moral issues were a real problem. I did occasionally meet up with the cadets – I didn't want to be unfriendly – but generally if I had free time and no pending test I would go out with my friends from church.

In the end, all my swotting and dedication paid off. Not only did I pass, the Lord encouraged me as I was commended by the lecturer in front of the whole class for getting excellent grades in anatomy and physiology. The following year was wonderful – I loved the work, though it was physically very hard. How often I had to bathe my aching feet! They went beyond tired to being painful.

For several years, I had been going to the Keswick Convention with the youth group from my church, which I loved doing. I must record what happened at Keswick when I was 19, I think. We had gone for a missions week and we watched a film about five young men who had been killed trying to reach a remote tribe in the rainforest in Ecuador. It moved me deeply and I found myself thinking: Could the Lord use someone like me, with all my limitations and lack of education?

We were all challenged to think hard and pray for what God wanted to do in our lives. I remember thinking I would love to serve the Lord in that land and I began to pray quite earnestly. On the last day, we were invited to stand to show our willingness to follow the Lord's will and, much to my surprise, someone said from the front: 'What about taking the place of one of those young men in Ecuador?'

I could not stay in my seat, I had to stand! I sensed the

Lord saying, 'Don't be afraid of being limited. Just let me equip you to do my will.' This was a very significant moment in my life: it made me all the more determined to complete my three-year training as a nurse.

I had just begun my second year and was working on the orthopaedic ward when an older lady came in. I knew her at once – she was from the village where I grew up. Mrs Downs had quite crippling rheumatoid arthritis. She had fallen and fractured her femur, and just 'stabilising' her leg and putting it in traction was very painful for her.

As soon as I could, I went over to her and reassured her that her pain would slowly go. She asked, 'Do I know you?' 'Of course you do,' I said, 'I'm Brenda from number 26.' 'Ha!', she cried, 'You're that lovely man Bill Hughes's daughter!' We had a good chat and I promised to see her later when I was off-duty so I could catch up with her and all the news.

When I finished work the next day, I stayed behind to visit Mrs Downs. At first I found her rather unhappy – she was complaining a lot, which I put down to her discomfort. I knew she had had a reputation for being rather grumpy even when I was little, but I thought that I mustn't let that affect the care I gave her, so I just listened to her and tried to be really kind. She proved very hard to please. The other nurses found her rude and demanding, and she would often swear at them.

A few weeks after Mrs Downs was admitted, I was put on night duty for a month on that ward. I wanted to win her confidence and fortunately I was able to do some little extras to help her. She talked to me about a daughter and two grandsons who lived in East Anglia and I did manage to develop a deeper relationship with her.

She knew that I had gone to church in Cutsyke and one night she said to me: 'You Christians get on my nerves. My daughter was a Salvationist and then she met this chap from East Anglia who belongs to the Brethren and she left us all to marry him and live down south. Her family should come first!'

I was a bit shocked by what she had said and didn't know how to respond. I asked, 'Do you see her and your grandsons?' 'Not as much as I should,' she replied. 'My grandsons are really nice young fellows, but like their mum they are too religious!'

Several nights later, she brought up the subject of her daughter again. It seems she had visited her the previous day and the younger of her grandsons had sent her a card or a letter. Mrs Downs seemed to be a little happier and she asked me to come to see her when I had finished my shift.

She asked me then: 'Do you have time to help me write my grandson a letter?' Her hand was deformed by arthritis and she couldn't hold a pen. So, I became her secretary: she dictated and I wrote down verbatim what she said. At the end of her letter, I added a line of my own to tell him I had known his grandma since I was little and I was so pleased she was getting in touch with him.

My time on nights was finished, so it was daytime when I was next in the ward. It seems that Mrs Downs had told her daughter all about me, and when she came at visiting time she asked if I was on duty. I was, and so we met and talked about her mother. She thanked me for making the effort to befriend her – her mother had a very bitter view of life in general, she told me sadly. 'We all know that she has suffered a lot of pain, so we try hard to help her. You seem to have won her trust and we are grateful. She told me that you're a committed Christian – I shall pray for you.'

The next time I was on duty, Mrs Downs called to me excitedly: 'I have a letter for you from my grandson. That's just like Boy John, he's such a kind lad!'

John Hart – or 'Boy John' to his family – was two years younger than me and had written to thank me for helping his grandma send her letter. At the end he asked:

'Would you write to me again and tell me about your life as a nurse and about your church?'

I did write, and we continued to correspond with each other for quite a long time. We were both involved in our churches in similar ways and so we encouraged each other, and naturally we shared news about family and work as well.

In 1958, in my second year, we had the most awful epidemic of what was called 'the Asian flu'. It was the worst dose of flu the country had suffered in a long time. The hospital staff, too, were going down with it, which meant that those of us who remained on our feet had a really heavy workload. I was so thankful that so far I had escaped – the fact that I had very scarred lungs from pulmonary TB meant that I would be very sick if I got a chest infection.

The epidemic seemed to be abating and nursing life was getting back to normal when I started to feel very unwell. When I got home from my shift, all I wanted to do was go to bed. At first I thought it was just fatigue from working so hard. I took some paracetamol and told my sister that I didn't feel too good and would sleep on if I could as I had the next day off.

I got little sleep that night! My head was pounding and my whole body was hurting; I could feel my temperature rising and I knew that I had the dreaded flu. My condition got steadily worse, until I was having difficulty breathing.

In the morning, Dad called the doctor from the phone box outside our house. He came late that afternoon and gave me some pills for the pain and something else to bring down the fever, and told Dad to ring him if I got any worse in the night. Well, I did get much worse in the night. I became delirious and could hardly breathe, gasping for air.

Dad summoned the doctor, who quickly phoned for an ambulance. He believed I had double pneumonia and

I needed to be in a steam tent and have antibiotics. I had become an emergency, though I think I was far too sick to know what was happening. All my friends at the hospital – nurses and junior doctors – were very concerned for me as I was put on the dangerously-ill list. My family were extremely worried.

After a week or so, my condition began to improve, though it was very slow going. I spent three weeks in hospital and even when I was discharged, my GP had to monitor my progress. I was soon longing to get back to my work and my studies, but he said that I had to be patient, because my lungs were still not fully recovered.

I was feeling very sorry for myself as I thought this had spoilt my chances of becoming a nurse. I made an early appointment to talk to my GP, who was a fatherly man, very kind but also straight to the point. Dr White knew our family well and thought highly of my dad, whose doctor he had been for most of his life.

'Brenda,' he told me, 'you are a very fortunate young lady – you are on the mend. But it's going to take time to get you fully recovered and you will have to put your nurse's training on hold for at least six months. You nearly died, be grateful! I realise that this is a huge disappointment, but you are still young and I know you will recover from this, too.'

I asked: 'Am I not able to work at all?' He said: 'If you can get an undemanding job so that at least you are earning and not bored, that would be good. Have a look at the Pontefract liquorice factory, something gentle like that. You wouldn't be breathing in any infections there.'

To say that I was disappointed is an understatement. I was plunged deep into doubt and gripped by sorrow – it was almost like a physical pain. I found very little comfort in God's word. Had I mistaken my calling? Who was I to think that the Lord could use someone like me? Would I ever get back into nursing and become a missionary? My mind was restless and my heart was deeply distressed.

My dad saw all of this and grieved with me. How loving and kind he was, and so were Marlene and her new husband, John! They couldn't fully comprehend my spiritual struggles because they didn't know the Saviour as I did or understand what a call to serve him meant to me; but nevertheless they were full of concern and sympathy.

Then something happened that – I can see as I look back – slowly and gently changed my life.

Chapter 5

After I had been discharged from hospital, I got a letter from John in East Anglia wanting to know why I hadn't answered his latest letters. I think they must have been misplaced – the weeks of my illness had been a bit of a haze, really. He asked: Did I want him to keep writing?

I wrote him a long reply telling him all that had happened, and explained that I was floundering in my walk with the Lord. I had never told him about my call to Ecuador as a missionary – it was too private and sensitive – but I had mentioned my consuming desire to serve the Lord. I also told John what the doctor had said and that I was about to try for a job at the liquorice factory until I was properly fit.

I got a reply within days. What encouraged me in his letter was that he told me he had shown mine to his mother and they both promised to pray for me.

My church friends were very caring, too, and I had some time with one of the leaders and that was also a great support.

The next time I saw my doctor, I was able to tell him that I was starting at the liquorice factory the following week, in the sweet-selection department. I remember that Mary Lamb, who lived next door to us, worked at the factory as well.

In the early spring of 1960, I got a letter from John, enclosing one also from his mum (who turned out to be the sister of Hilda, my lovely supervisor at the clothing factory). She invited me to come and stay with them for a holiday in their lovely Suffolk village.

John's letter as always was a treat to receive! He, too, was keen for me to come and stay. At first, however, I felt a bit uncomfortable about the idea of going down to East Anglia. I hadn't even been out of Yorkshire except for the six months I had spent in Croydon and I worried that these people would find me very different from them.

Like most northerners, I was an outgoing person – it seems to be part of our culture. I loved the people of North Yorkshire: mainly farming people, down to earth, hard-working and tough, very much like the mining people of West Yorkshire.

I let Dad read the letters and we talked things over. 'Brenda,' he said, 'don't miss this opportunity to meet different people! I thought you wanted to nurse abroad. How strange would that be in comparison?'

He certainly had a point. Marlene and her husband and Maurice, too, all urged me to go. In the end, it was agreed that I would go at the beginning of August for the two weeks when the factory was closed.

I should say that my dad had a thing about his daughters and boyfriends. He had always told me quite straight if he thought any chap was unsuitable – and so far he hadn't met one who passed muster. Whenever I brought someone home, his comment was: 'Sorry, Brenda, he's not for you!'

Poor Marlene had been put through the mill over her John – but then she was only 19 or 20 when she married and here I was, 22 and I had never had a long-term boyfriend. There was another problem, I realised: I was vetting any potential admirer myself for their interest in foreign mission! There had been one boy who I fell in love with, but he was not really interested in serving the Lord and so I had had to break with him completely.

It was a real learning curve for me, and quite painful.

Going to work in a factory once again was not the big disappointment I had expected. I made lots of new friends and was able to persuade them to come to church with me. Maybe four or five of them started coming regularly and joined the youth group, and all of these found the Lord as their Saviour.

One was my next-door neighbour Mary Lamb; another was a girl called Sheila. Those two were very dear friends to me. They both married really nice Christian boys.

My doctor told me he was more and more pleased with my improving health. He thought I would get back to nursing eventually but I should see how I coped with the coming winter.

August approached, and my trip to Suffolk to stay with the Harts. John and I had been writing often and, as we had no photos of ourselves to send each other, I told him I was five foot six and slim, with long, dark brown, wavy hair. I said I would be wearing a bright blue coat, and John gave me the registration number of their Austin Ruby, which I would find in the station car park.

The big day arrived at last. Marlene and her husband took me to the station and I was on my way. My destination was Thetford, which is just inside Norfolk. I have very little recollection of the journey, though it took almost a whole day. I remember that I had to change trains once.

Then, all of a sudden, I was there, getting off the train and making for the car park. John was standing on a bridge to see me get off and he recognised me at once from the description I had given him.

I found the right car and had been standing there for a few minutes, in some trepidation, when I saw this very slim, blond man walking towards me with a smile on his face. That can't be him, I thought – in my imagination he was much taller and had dark hair. He stuck out his hand and said: 'You're Brenda, I presume.' We shook hands and I said, 'And you are Dr Livingstone?' That got a laugh, which eased the tension somewhat.

A few steps behind him were a couple of close friends he had brought along with him as he was feeling so shy about meeting this Yorkshire girl, who he thought he knew from the letters I had written to him but who was actually still a stranger.

'You must have guessed I'm John,' he said. 'Welcome to East Anglia!'

The drive to his house took 30 or 40 minutes, maybe. I remember I made them all laugh when I mistook some sugar beet for strange-looking cabbages. We dropped his friends, Ron and Janet, off and then had about 15 minutes to go to the next village, Hopton, where John lived.

I told him, with a bit of a cheeky grin: 'You don't look a bit like I imagined you. I pictured you as tall, dark and handsome!' He laughed and said: 'To be honest, until you told me otherwise I thought you were a dainty blonde.' I found out later that his mum had already described me, so he was teasing me. (I was only two inches shorter than John – in those days I was considered very tall for a woman!)

Mrs Hart was delighted that I had made the trip. She knew I had been very ill and she was very concerned about my health.

When we turned into their drive, John's dad was in the yard waiting. I jumped out of the car to say hello and he came up close, inspected me and asked me if I was wearing face powder! I was taken aback. I had never worn make-up, but only because I couldn't afford it – Marlene did and so did a lot of my friends and I thought they looked nice in it. John was a bit put out by the question but just passed it off with an 'Oh, Dad!'

He had two brothers. Joseph, the eldest, lived with his wife in a small town nearby. David was just 18 months older than John and had just got engaged to a young woman who lived next-door – also named Brenda!

My Yorkshireness was something that David found difficult, and at times amusing. What came across was that I seemed uneducated to him, and he would make jokes that made me feel uncomfortable and put down.

However, I felt really accepted by everyone else I met on that holiday. John's friends were real, down-to-earth country people. Ron and Janet were newly married and were such dear, sincere people. I also met Ron's brother Cliff and his wife, Maureen, who were a few years older than us and had small children.

John had taken time off work while I was staying at his house. He was a trainee sanitary inspector, but when he was alone with me he told me he disliked his job but had yet to break it to his parents that he wanted to be a nurse!

We went to meetings together at various local Brethren churches. John was often the speaker and I was very impressed by how accomplished he was, when he was only just into his twenties.

He had been teaching for some weeks at one of these churches on the life of Abraham and it amused us that the week he took me the subject was how Abraham sent his servant to find a wife for his son Isaac and how Rebekah said yes, she was willing to marry him before she had even met him!

We went for long drives in the beautiful, flat countryside. The houses in Norfolk and Suffolk were painted lovely shades of deep terracotta, pink and cream, and a lot of them had thatched roofs, which I loved. I was especially enchanted by the Abbey Gardens in Bury St Edmunds, the town where John worked, just 13 miles from Hopton.

We spent time with his family. Most of the time I was happy getting to know them better, but there were tensions between John and David, who was a really strong character who knew his own mind and expressed it quite forcefully. On one occasion, an argument at the table between him and John made their mother cry. That made me think that there was a sense of competition between them.

John and I loved to just walk and talk, and I so enjoyed his company! I was impressed most of all by his gentle manner. A number of his friends had come to know the Saviour partly because of John's loving ways with them.

As time passed, John and I recognised that much of our thinking was spiritually in tune. However, I sensed that he wanted a romantic relationship and somehow I held back, as I tended to do when I had found a good male friend who was a Christian.

Towards the end of my second week in Suffolk, John asked me plainly if I had any interest in him at all. I thought this was my chance to talk about my call to be a missionary in Ecuador.

I asked him whether he had seen the film *Mid-Century Martyrs* and he responded very warmly. 'Well,' I said, 'since I was 19 I have had a call from the Lord to be a missionary in Ecuador. One of the reasons I haven't become involved with anyone is that I can't deny my call, so naturally I'm reluctant to commit to anyone until I know where they're going with regard to God's will for their life.'

John was visibly affected by my words. He took my hand and said: 'I want to show you something when we get home.'

He proceeded to tell me that not only had he seen the film but he had heard a missionary from the Brethren church in Bury St Edmunds explain why and how the deaths of those five young men had happened (he had worked with them personally for some years). At the end, the missionary had looked into the congregation and said, with some emotion – pointing, John felt, at him – 'What about you, young man? Would you give your life as a missionary to Ecuador?'

'Well,' John said, 'I certainly told the Lord that night I was willing, and I've written it in my journal.'

We were both near to tears. Immediately, it had made me think that God might be bringing us together for his service – and yet I felt that we must still be careful. I was quiet and pensive, when John said: 'I'm going to tell you something I had no intention of telling you before.

'When I saw you get off the train, I had an inner conviction that you were to be my wife. At first, it was almost irrational to have such a thought, but as I've come to know you more deeply, and after all we have talked about, I've come to feel with all my heart that you are the sort of girl I've been looking for.'

I was at a loss to know how to respond. In fact, I was a bit stunned. After a while, I laughed and said: 'We've known each other for two weeks and we don't know each other well enough to make that kind of decision. You hope to get into nursing, I want to get back into nursing, so let's be very good friends, as we have been, and get to know each other better.'

Then I went on: 'Until the doctor gives me the go-ahead, I have to stay home – but maybe I could come and spend Christmas with you?'

In the months until Christmas, John motored up to see me in Yorkshire a couple of times. That ancient Austin Ruby would be steaming hot and gasping by the time he arrived!

My family pulled out all the stops to make him feel welcome. Marlene was slightly in awe of this chap with what she called 'a BBC accent' and laughingly told him: 'You sound very posh. I hope you can understand our lingo.' 'Marlene,' he said, 'I'll have you know I'm half Yorkshire and proud of it!'

John was staying with his cousin Geoff, who lived on the same housing estate as us, so at the end of that first evening, off he went.

After he had gone, Marlene, John and Maurice were all very outspoken about him. 'Well,' they said, 'so you've found yourself a toff, have you?' (This sort of attitude was quite common in Yorkshire.) 'He is far from being a toff,' I retorted. 'He and his family are just like us.'

Dad had been very quiet and he didn't say anything until we were alone. 'Brenda,' he told me then, 'this young man is the sort of man I've always envisioned for you. He is a gentleman; his sort are few on the ground. I hope it all works out for you.'

On Sunday we went to my church, where he met most of my Christian friends in one big day of fellowship. Of course, some of the older people had known his grandma, Mrs Downs, and one or two were sure they remembered his mum as a child. It was such a happy day. How we laughed and talked! We so enjoyed the love and friendship of people who truly knew God.

My lovely factory girls, too, were so glad to meet John. He was staying until Tuesday, so he arranged to come on Monday at five to pick me and Mary up from work. I introduced him to all my friends (some of whom he had seen in church anyway) and when we drove off, they were jumping about like kids – the Austin Ruby had made a hit!

Chapter 6

Christmas came and I made my second trip to Suffolk. I was very excited to be spending more time with John and his family, and also with Ron and Janet, Cliff and Maureen and their children. It was good, too, to meet other friends of John's, such as his old friend Eric and his new wife, Pam. They lived in Bury St Edmunds and were to be such good, faithful friends to us when we were studying there.

Naturally, John and I needed time to ourselves, so we would wrap up warm and go out walking for miles, talking and sharing deeply.

My GP had seen me a few weeks earlier and he was now encouraging me to look at resuming my training as a nurse. In fact, I was resolved to start it again, from scratch. John and I discussed whether I should return to my own hospital in Yorkshire, where I was known and would be welcomed back, or should try to get into West Suffolk General in Bury St Eds.

I knew that the spring intake was already full – with John enrolled among them – but I could apply to be in the next one. John confided that he felt rather scared at the prospect of starting his training as a nurse; but I told him he would be fine – the men I had worked with were accepted and highly valued.

We were always encouraging each other. I felt so drawn to this fine man, for the first time I was able to let the romance of what was happening to me blossom.

John suggested that I should look for a temporary job in East Anglia for a month or so and then I could put in my application to West Suffolk General. We didn't make a firm decision but resolved to think and pray about it. It would be such a life change for me, and the idea of being so far away from my family and friends in Yorkshire was quite frightening to me, to say the least. There were people in the local churches who made me feel quite uncomfortable and inferior to them.

When I got home to Castleford and returned to work, I settled down to seeking direction for the not-too-distant future. Dad thought I should take my time. He also told me to go and ask one of the elders in the church, who had known and loved me since I was in Sunday school.

About a month into the new year, I went to see two of the elders, Mr Ritson and Mr Wallbank – but not together, as I thought that the Lord would make things clearer with two separate opinions. As it happened, they both said the same thing: they thought John and I were made for each other and I should go to be nearer to him.

Both of them added that it would be a loss to the church and they would miss me enormously. The three of us came together to pray and it was quite emotional! The two elders asked that God's will would be done in our lives, and they promised with hugs to continue to pray for me and John and take an interest in our future.

After thinking things through, I came to the conclusion that, with their guidance and kind support, I now needed to trust the Lord completely and go to East Anglia. I wrote to John and told him how things had gone, and he was very excited! Obviously, he had hoped I would join him, but he hadn't wanted to put any pressure on me, as he truly looked for God's direction.

The next few weeks were hectic. I handed in my notice at the factory and the church arranged a surprise farewell, followed by an amazing party! I had asked John to find out whether there was any work going in the area, ideally as a live-in nanny or something like that, so that I could be financially independent. Within a week or so, I got a letter from him telling me that there were a few jobs available in the nanny department, so all I had to do was to book my tickets and pack my things.

It was a fine spring day in April 1961 when I set off for

East Anglia. I felt very sad to be leaving behind my dad and the rest of my family, my many friends and my church. It was hard for me, and in some ways a little scary, but I put myself in the Lord's hands and I knew I could always trust him to help me.

I felt a tingle of excitement as my train drew into Thetford, to meet John again and start a whole new life.

The arrangement was that I would stay with John's parents until I found work. Amazingly, I got a job almost immediately, looking after a girl of four. It looked ideal: her parents were farmers and her mother was seven months pregnant, and they knew I was hoping to return to training as a nurse. I was to start at the end of May and live with them.

The work was quite pleasant. Little Magdalene was not too difficult, she just needed to get to know me, and with time we became the best of friends.

The only downside was that the farm was way out in the sticks, maybe 15 or 20 miles from Bury St Eds. Buses into town were few, and many of them didn't go as far as I needed in the evenings. Unfortunately, that meant that I didn't see John very often. He was still in PTS at the hospital and so he had the weekends free, and on a couple of occasions he managed to borrow the Austin Ruby and come to see me. Apart from that, we just kept writing letters to each other.

I applied to the hospital and succeeded in getting into the next intake, to start in early September. All went to plan and I left the farm towards the end of August. At last, John and I could have a proper relationship!

He had settled well into PTS and was really enjoying it. He had told all his set about me and they became good friends to me, right through our training together. I know of only one woman among them who was a Christian, but they were all forever encouraging us, and in some ways were our champions.

Every hospital in East Anglia had its own PTS and so the numbers studying together in each of them were very small. This made the whole experience friendlier than the one I had had in Harrogate. My set was a really great group – no more than a dozen strong, including two from Trinidad and a couple of Irish girls. There were two men and they were such fun – they livened things up a lot!

John was not allowed in the nurses' home and I was not allowed in the men's accommodation, though we sometimes met in the grounds of the hospital. He was now on shifts but we managed to see each other fairly often. The big problem was where to go. John had a married cousin living in town, whose four-year-old son was profoundly deaf. What a character he was! We visited them often – the three Rs, Rose, Ray and little Richard – and he would keep us all on our toes.

There was also John's friends Eric and Pam to see.

It was harder to synchronise our times off once I had finished PTS and was onto ward duty, but we did manage to have some great times together. John had never even been to the pictures before he met me! As we got to know each other better, we realised that we had quite different personalities. I thought that he was too intense at times and he thought I was sometimes too easygoing and didn't take things as seriously as I should.

He observed that my sense of humour was a good thing but that it seemed I saw the funny side of things much more than he did. John taught me to think more deeply and I taught him to laugh more. Occasionally we would have a misunderstanding, but we always tried to sort things out quickly and keep communicating.

I had been on the wards a few months when Matron (who was a committed Christian) asked us to go and see her. She thought there should be a Christian fellowship at the hospital and she knew that John and I were friends and were both believers. As it happened, he and I had been thinking that we should try to spread the good news around the hospital and had been contemplating forming some kind of group with other Christians.

Matron told us how to get in touch with the Hospital Christian Fellowship for guidance. This was a country-wide inter-hospital association and it was really helpful. To some extent, though, we learnt bit by bit by getting together as a group of Christians and working hard alongside each other. Slowly, things started to happen.

There was also a student nurses' association at the hospital which we joined, and we began to lend a hand in some of their activities, too.

One thing we soon noticed was the excessive drinking at some of the association's social events, and especially the dances. We Christians went along, but in order to look out for women who might be vulnerable, to make sure they got back safely to the nurses' home. Some would be rather unwell, even actually vomiting, so we helped them, too, and in time we became quite well known as 'the rescue mob'!

After a while, John had the idea of doing a nightly epilogue on the hospital radio, which came to be really appreciated. We introduced Christian music and patients started to put in requests for a favourite hymn.

All in all, John and I had very full lives. What with our studies, our really demanding work schedules, church and family, we might easily have been unable to find any time to relax and to be on our own together. So, we made sure that we got the occasional weekend off together, and we would go to stay with John's parents or visit friends from our Brethren church in Bury St Eds. We loved that church – at that time we had little input, but we were well supported and cared for.

We got engaged in the late summer of 1962, in an informal little ceremony in the church at Cutsyke in front of an invited audience of family, close friends from the church and a few of the elders. It was all my idea – I was full of ideas! We exchanged rings, as I gave John a signet ring with his initials JGH in fancy lettering, which he would always love.

Dad was so thrilled that I was going to marry him, and the rest of the family were happy for us, too. So were my old church friends – Mary and Sheila were delighted when I asked them to be my bridesmaids.

We had to wait to get married until John at least was qualified, as we received only token wages as student nurses – we were earning £9 a month, although we did get our living-in free. I started putting money aside for the wedding and John began to save up for a suit and the honeymoon.

The first time I went to look at the wedding dresses in the bridal store in Bury St Eds, I saw a man who had been a patient of mine some time before. 'Are you getting married?', he asked me. 'Yes,' I said. 'Are you?' 'No,' he replied, 'I own the shop!' He told me that if I was buying a dress, he might be able to give me a discount.

It took a few visits before I found exactly the dress I wanted – a beautiful, plain white dress that was just me. When I went to pay, the owner said with a twinkle in his eye: 'This is a gift from me to you. Have a wonderful wedding!'

I am so grateful to that man – his kindness made such a difference! All the money I had been saving for my dress we were able to put to other uses.

We were married in Cutsyke on the 30th November 1963. I will try to convey what an unusual wedding it was.

Knowing my family situation, Matron had advised me to save some of my leave so that I could go home well in advance to sort out the reception and all the other elements of a wedding. Not having a mother and with Dad being so sick and frail and living a bus ride away from the church made things really difficult for me.

Accordingly, I was back in Castleford two weeks before the day. The ladies of the church were a huge help to me and so was my sister – but I had to be there.

The Brethren in Cutsyke had built a new church next to the old, familiar one (in which we were going to have our reception). The new church was very new and, with less than a week to go until the wedding, the floor still had to be painted. This caused me a lot of concern, as time was running out.

We decided that a cold meal would be best and that it could be sorted out on the day, as long as the tables had all been laid the night before. We lived a good half an hour away from the church by bus and I had to get the first bus of the day for us to sort the food and plate it up. So, things were a bit manic...

The weather could not have been worse: there was a dense fog and the bus was late. Still, Marlene and I got to the church in the end. The ladies had made a start and we did all that had to be done so that I could get home to get myself ready to be married.

The fog still had not lifted and the traffic was terrible. As soon as Marlene and I got back, I had a bath and then piled up my long hair in the new bouffant style. When I had finished dressing, I put on my veil. I had made this myself: it was fastened to an Alice band and I had stuck little diamantés to it and it looked really lovely. The bridesmaids were ready, the photos at the house were done and off the bridesmaids went. Dad and I were to follow almost immediately in a chauffeur-driven car.

As soon as we were on the road, we realised that the fog was creating havoc. Also, we learnt from the driver, there was a big rugby match on in Leeds. What a nightmare the journey was! The traffic crawled and my lovely dad was almost in tears for my sake. 'Dad,' I said, 'this is a great day, please don't get upset! You are with me, the Lord is with me and I'm going to marry the finest man on earth!'

He kissed me and told me he loved me very much. He also said: 'Your mother is here with us. I can feel her.'

We arrived more than an hour late and Dad proudly walked me up the aisle, to be joined in marriage to my beloved John. We made our entrance to the hymn 'O the deep, deep love of Jesus!':

> O the deep, deep love of Jesus!
> Vast, unmeasured, boundless, free,
> Rolling as a mighty ocean
> In its fullness over me.
> Underneath me, all around me,
> Is the current of thy love;
> Leading onward, leading homeward,
> To thy glorious rest above.
>
> O the deep, deep love of Jesus!
> Spread his praise from shore to shore;
> How he loveth, ever loveth,
> Changeth never, nevermore;
> How he watches o'er his loved ones,
> Died to call them all his own;
> How for them he intercedeth,
> Watcheth o'er them from the throne.
>
> O the deep, deep love of Jesus!
> Love of ev'ry love the best:
> 'Tis an ocean vast of blessing,
> 'Tis a haven sweet of rest.
> O the deep, deep love of Jesus!
> 'Tis a heav'n of heav'ns to me;
> And it lifts me up to glory,
> For it lifts me up to thee.

How our lives together were to prove the truth of those words! As the years passed, John and I would fail each other many times, but the love of Jesus never failed us.

John had a broad smile on his face and looked so happy!

The service was lovely, and then we were pronounced 'man and wife'. I looked at my husband and I could not stop smiling – we were now together for the rest of our lives.

We went into a side room to sign the register, and found that the floor was still wet with paint. It made a sticky red mess of the hem of my dress. At the time I was just so elated that it didn't matter, but later I had the dress cleaned professionally as a number of my nursing friends wanted to use it.

At the reception, unfortunately, there were a few gatecrashers – distant relatives of mine – which put us all in a spin as there were not enough chairs or settings. The photos were soon done – in the church, as the weather was still awful.

We didn't hang around afterwards as we had a long journey to make, south to Bournemouth. My friend Philip Fryer was going back to university and had asked us for a lift part of the way, and John's very close friend Don Aiken wanted a lift, too.

John had been lent a car by a couple he knew in the church in Bury St Eds. It was large and roomy, so we could all travel in comfort. When we stopped off at a petrol station to fill up, the attendant was amazed to see not one man but three get out of an obvious 'just married' car, still wearing their buttonholes. 'Wow!', he said. 'Which one of you is the bridegroom?' In unison, all the lads said 'Me!', which only made us laugh more.

We made good time and dropped Philip and Don off where they needed to be, but when we took a look at how much further we had to go, we were dismayed to find that we were still miles away from Bournemouth. It was very late by now and we were exhausted, and John was finding the driving difficult as a result.

We decided to find a bed-and-breakfast to stay in and eventually we found one with a vacant room – in the attic. It was a very cold night and the room was icy, so John gallantly went down to see if we could have a hot-water bottle. When he got to the ground floor, a little Yorkshire terrier jumped out from somewhere and nipped him!

When he finally got back to the attic, he was surprised to find me already in bed. He made fun of the situation, but I said: 'I'm so tired and cold! Hurry up and get in with me with that bottle!' – which he did, with a lot of giggling.

We had a fairly good night but, anxious to get to warmth and comfort, we made a very early start and arrived at our Christian guest house in Bournemouth in time to freshen up and have lunch.

We had been there only a couple of days when John met someone he knew who was there on holiday. This man told the management that John was a speaker in Suffolk and the next thing we knew he was being asked to do some of the daily talks!

Don was doing a children's holiday club not far away, so we arranged to drive out one day and meet up with him and his team. We enjoyed it so much that we did it again.

How wonderful our honeymoon was! We were ecstatic just being together, with no one and nothing to stop us being close to each other. We were so full of gratitude to our heavenly Father for bringing us together, and we prayed that our marriage would bring glory to our Lord.

Chapter 7

We couldn't afford to rent a house or a flat, so instead we took a static caravan on a site not far from the hospital in Bury St Eds.

John had finished his training a few months before we got married and in the new year the hospital offered him a job as the staff nurse on the orthopaedic ward. They wanted him to be trained up to take over as the charge nurse in due course, as the man who was currently in post was shortly to retire.

We had talked about starting a family soon. In the Sixties, it was thought that the older you were, the more likely you were to encounter problems in your first pregnancy – and at 26 I was already considered 'elderly'! Before long, I was expecting a baby.

In due course, I sat my finals and passed them.

One day in July, Matron summoned us to give us the good news that we were to be offered a hospital house on a new housing estate. Wow, we were so excited – and very grateful! We moved in in August. I remember that it was very hot all that week and I felt the heat badly, but it didn't spoil the fun we had going to secondhand-furniture stores – we had nothing!

We got the immediate necessities, such as a table and chairs. The bed and the dressing table we bought new, but I made bedside tables out of wooden orange-boxes covered with pretty material and they looked lovely and cheerful.

Once we were settled, we invited my dad to come and stay for a couple of months. John was really fond of him and I loved seeing them together. Dad was not a Christian, so John would take him out to the pub and spend time with him. He treated him with great respect and they really bonded.

Some time later, my old church in Cutsyke decided to

do a children's mission in Airedale (where my dad was still living) and asked John to be the speaker. We both went up to Yorkshire for it and it was a great week in every way. The most wonderful thing that happened was that my dad went every evening and towards the end of the week he told John that he wanted to be like a little child and accept the Saviour – which he did. Our joy knew no bounds!

I worked full-time until the beginning of October, but then I started getting swollen ankles, so we decided that I should reduce my hours. One day in the second week of November, as I was walking to work, I suddenly felt very dizzy and faint. I leant against a lamp post and a passer-by saw what was up and flagged down a motorist, who quickly got me to A&E.

John was called from his ward and was with me when I was told that I had serious toxaemia and would have to be admitted for bed rest. I had a condition known as 'pre-eclampsia', which involves high blood pressure leading to kidney problems. Apparently, my blood pressure was very high. Unfortunately, I now had to remain in hospital until my baby was born – it was due between the 20th and 25th December.

The weeks passed slowly, but I was an avid reader and I knitted and, of course, conversed with the other patients and the staff. John would pop in all the time, as he was able to do, though unfortunately I never saw him for long enough to have a deep conversation with him. Neither of us could know how well or otherwise the other was coping with the situation, and towards the end John seemed remote and preoccupied, not himself at all.

My set had its graduation ceremony in late November. I kept bothering the nurses about this, as I wanted to be there; eventually, one of the doctors asked the consultant and I was told that I could go if my blood pressure was OK on the day.

When the day arrived, my BP was fine, so the hairdresser came and did my hair beautifully and I was all ready to go when my BP was taken again. Evidently it had shot up to a dangerous level, for the doctor forbade me to go. I was so disappointed! However, I knew that he was right to be on the safe side, so I tried to be brave about it and not make a fuss.

I was induced into labour, and Mary Jane was born, two days before Christmas 1964. John was with me at the birth and was given her to hold, and then I held her. What a precious gift to us she was – and she has always been so, the most wonderful of daughters!

I called her 'Mary Jane' – John was to leave the naming of all our children to me – because some of my nicest childhood friends were called Mary and 'Jane' is the feminine version of 'John'.

As you can imagine, after six weeks in hospital I was fired up to be going home. The day came for my discharge and it was arranged that John would come for me in the afternoon. I was so excited! I had a beautiful, healthy new baby, I was well myself and I was to be home with my dear husband once more.

It was evening when John collected me and on the journey home he was very subdued and seemed to be unhappy about something. We were soon at the door and John picked up the carrycot with the baby inside and I followed him into the house. He put the carrycot on the dining-room table and then sort of stood there. He was really strange and distant, no hugs and no 'Welcome home!' He said: 'Well, take off your coat then!' To say I was puzzled and hurt is an understatement. I felt devastated. What had happened to him during those weeks by himself?

He took his own coat off and went upstairs, while I made myself a cup of tea and sat with Mary Jane, choking back the tears. She was fast asleep and John hadn't come down, so I went up to look for him and found him taking a bath. The way he was treating me gave me such pain, I couldn't say anything; I went back downstairs and started to sort things out for the night for the baby and myself.

She was going to sleep in the carrycot while she was small, so I called John to ask him to take it upstairs. He did so in silence. When I had finished feeding Mary Jane, I went up and put her in the cot in our bedroom. I found John already in bed. 'What's the matter?', I asked him. 'Are you unwell?' He said: 'No, I'm just very tired.'

What a dreadful night I had! I was deeply wounded by his strange behaviour and very confused. John had to go to work the next day, so there was little chance of finding out then what was going on.

In fact, I never did find out. John just insisted that he was tired and I realised that I would have to give things over to the Lord, ask him for help and comfort and leave it there.

Life did become a little more normal as time went by. John was a little more natural, less aloof – but he was still far from how he had been before I went into hospital. There was a melancholy about him and he seemed less candid, more evasive. The fun and friendship we used to enjoy seemed to have vanished.

I grieved for the man I had known and was nagged by doubt. What could have caused him to behave like that? Was he regretting being married and having responsibility for a baby?

His workload was heavy – he had a tendency to take on more and more things on top of a demanding job – and he wore himself out. He didn't eat properly, lost weight and began having asthma attacks. He was often quite distant.

My life was very different, too. I had a lovely little baby to care for and a big house to keep clean and tidy, but I had no hoover, no washing machine, no fridge, and we lived a long way from town. It was a new housing estate, there were very few buses and I didn't know anyone.

I had no family locally to go and visit, no mother to guide and encourage me or sister nearby to turn to, no really close friend to confide in. Our nearest neighbours were out at work Monday to Friday. I did try to make friends, but with very little success.

Because I was a nurse, it was assumed that I would be fine looking after a new baby, but in fact I felt inadequate. It worried me how frustrated I would get at times when I was caring for Mary Jane and things didn't go quite to plan. She was an easy baby on the whole, but inevitably there were difficult times and then I felt very lost, abandoned and oh, so lonely! I found it hard to bear.

My whole life had changed. Before, I had had so many friends, John and I had done so much together – right up until I went into hospital we had been such a team! – and the Hospital Christian Fellowship had given me so much joy and fulfilment.

Apart from his job as a charge nurse, John was involved in a long list of extra Christian activities: he had founded a local branch of the Gideons, he ran the HCF, he did nightly epilogues on the hospital radio and he spoke at local churches. With a friend he had founded a male voice choir, and he helped with the Sunday school on the estate we lived on.

Sadly, he was very rarely at home with me and the baby. I felt utterly neglected, frightened and confused. If I said anything to him about his absence, he would say: 'I'm serving the Lord, so you should be happy! Grumbling at me is just not helpful. Your place is here in the house, looking after Mary Jane.'

In anguish, I prayed for the Lord to help me. He became my confidant as I poured out my fears and my hurts to him. He was my refuge and solace and only became more so as time went on.

I read some very good Christian books, by well-known

authors, and I had some amazing times in my devotions while Mary Jane was sleeping. My heavenly Father kept me from breakdown and helped me to cope.

I had the occasional visit from some of our nurse friends. Tina Grief, Alwyn Procter and Mary Brown all came to see me, and some others, too, although it was difficult with the shifts they had to work. Their studies and church life, too, kept them very busy.

Alwyn remains a very good friend to this day – we've kept up with each other ever since by phone and letter.

In late 1965, John suffered bleeding from a stomach ulcer. The doctor told him he was starving himself. Also, his asthma had become a constant affliction. I was very concerned about his health.

How I prayed for my husband! I knew that his problem was really a spiritual one, but there seemed to be nothing I could do. Gradually, I began to realise that my Lord knew all about the situation, and so I took everything to him: all my fears, my weakness, the awful loneliness.

And the reply I kept getting was: 'Trust me, Brenda! I am in control and I will protect you from all harm. Everything about you, John and Mary Jane, your future as a family, is in my hands. In me you will have the victory. Go on trusting me!'

So many lovely promises from scripture kept coming my way, and my trust in the Lord grew, too.

That Christmas was very special to me. I knew that Mary Jane and I would be with John on his ward on Christmas Day but that I would be alone for the rest of the season, so I set myself some spiritual targets, to spend it with my Saviour.

A week before Christmas, I read and reread the Advent story in the scriptures and meditated on the amazing fact that our God had been made flesh in the person of his Son – all for us, for me! The huge scale of it began to hit me in a special way, more astounding than I had ever experienced before.

On Christmas Eve, I wrapped Mary Jane up really warm, put a little hot-water bottle in the pram and off we set, walking round the estate. As I went, I was praying for the people who lived there and taking note of how they were celebrating the birth of our Lord Jesus Christ. Some houses looked bright and festive; others didn't show much evidence of Christmas at all.

It was a lovely December night, quite cold but bearably so. As I walked, I noticed that the sky was spectacularly beautiful. I heard a lot of Christmas music, some well-known carols, some quite secular. I was so blessed by seeing, through people's windows, their family lives going on, and I prayed for those families.

As I made my way home, I was gripped profoundly by the wonder of Emmanuel. I sensed the Lord Jesus so close to me, almost as if he was walking with me and holding my hand. Tears of great joy flowed down my face. His love was all around me and all I could do was thank him, over and over and over again, for coming to earth and for being my Saviour.

This lovely, sweet experience carried me into the new year. I knew I had been wonderfully blessed.

I am not quite sure how far into 1966 we were – perhaps early spring? – when John found he was having difficulty swallowing and it was getting steadily worse. I begged him to see a doctor, as I wondered whether he had a stricture of the oesophagus. In the end he had no choice, because he had become unable to swallow his saliva.

When he came back, he was quite worried, because the doctor said he could actually see a lump in his throat. He was scheduled for an X-ray, which showed a definite obstruction, so he was put on the list for an operation.

Although it proved to be nothing sinister – it was only a cyst – the whole saga had been a real scare for us both.

It gave me an opportunity to tell John I was afraid that his lifestyle was very detrimental to his health and could he at least try to eat better, a little more regularly and a little more at each meal.

There was no doubt that he was quite debilitated for a few weeks after this. I wanted him to rest a bit more and not be dashing about all round the clock.

He promised to try, but unfortunately he seemed unable to manage his activities and he soon returned to the same old habits. By May, he was running about doing so much that we hardly saw each other from one day to the next. I was very saddened by his neglect of Mary Jane as well.

By now, I was becoming desperate about the state of our marriage. I felt so heartbroken one night that I wept in front of the Lord: 'Please help me to know what to do! Please guide me! Please give me the opportunity to bare my soul to John, to let him see what is happening to us!'

I also felt that I needed to talk to John about our original call to Ecuador, because he was being offered a big promotion at the hospital.

Chapter 8

I decided to have a straight talk with John, so I waited up
late until he came in after one of his evening shifts, when
our little girl was asleep. He was surprised to see me still
up as I always had to get up so early for Mary Jane. I
asked him if he would like a drink, but he told me he was
tired and needed to get to bed. 'Well, John,' I said in a
determined voice, 'tonight you are going to listen to me,
tired or not – and I've got lots to say!'

My tone made him uncomfortable, but he sat down
and said: 'OK, Brenda, I'm all ears.' Now, John had big
ears that rather stuck out and as he said this he raised
his hands and waggled them. I laughed, and some of the
strain I was feeling dissipated – but I was not going to be
put off!

I went to sit beside him and took his hand. 'John,' I
began, 'I'm desperately unhappy, I feel so defrauded! I
feel that I am on the very fringe of your life. You are so
distant and there is no friendship between us; I doubt
that you really love me. You have time for everyone and
everything except Mary Jane and me – it's like being
rejected day after day.

'When did you last pray with me, or share anything
spiritual with me? When did we last have a deep
conversation?'

As I was talking, I was getting tearful. 'What about our
call to Ecuador? All our godly aspirations to serve the
Lord together and the sense of unity it gave us?

'Since Mary Jane was born, you have been a different
person. She's well over a year old now and she hardly
knows you! And I don't know you, either. You're not the
man I married.' With that, I burst into tears.

John was more than upset – he was deeply troubled.
He put his arms around me and held me close, which
made me cry even more. In between my sobs, I asked

him: 'Do you still love me? Do you still want to be married to me?'

'Oh, Brenda,' he replied, 'I do love you. I wouldn't want to be married to any other woman. Please forgive me for being such a fool and getting things so very wrong!' He was actually crying himself, he was so distressed. 'I must be with you more and communicate better, Brenda,' he continued quietly, holding me tight. 'All you have said is true – I have been a terrible husband and father. Can you forgive me? May God forgive me for causing so much suffering!'

We talked a lot that night. We were connecting again, especially in the way we saw our present situation and our future. We went to bed eventually, after promising each other a new start.

A few days later, John said: 'About Ecuador: I know that it is definitely God's will for us to go there. I've been putting it off, I've wanted to ignore it, because I'm so accepted here and everyone makes such a lot of me. I've become very self-centred. I've acted selfishly towards you in my daily life, and my service for God has been more about me than about my Lord and Saviour.'

Hearing this, I felt so much happier! We were moving in the right direction once more. Life was going to be better.

In his concern and consideration for me and Mary Jane, John definitely changed – but his workload would be harder to sort out. He did cut back on things like the male voice choir, and later the Gideons; but now he had told our elders that we wanted to go to Ecuador he had to win support for such a venture, and that meant visiting many churches throughout East Anglia to raise our profile.

He also had meetings with Echoes of Service, the Brethren's missionary support agency, which had agreed to send us on the 'commendation' of our two churches in Cutsyke and Bury St Eds.

In August, I became pregnant again. It was a real blessing, and yet it proved very difficult. I hadn't suffered from morning sickness with Mary Jane, but this time I spent most of the nine months exhausted by vomiting. It was very debilitating and I lived with a deep sense of vulnerability and felt quite fragile emotionally. Mary Jane was now a very active toddler and kept me on my toes – not easy to cope with when I felt so weak!

John was kind and caring, but there was no let-up in his work, both secular and Christian. Extended family can be a great help at times like these, but I didn't have any nearby. Thankfully, I was once more able to cast myself on my gracious Lord, and in reality that was the best thing that could have happened.

On one occasion, Mary Brown took me to her father's house and put me to bed while she looked after Mary Jane. She was trying to be kind, but I knew instinctively that she thought I was a bit of a wimp, not quite the wife for someone as admirable as John, who, like others in the HCF, she kind of hero-worshipped.

Mary was only 19 and she wouldn't have had a clue about what I was going through, so I accepted her help with gratitude for the peace and rest I had that day, for which I truly thanked the Lord.

Once the new year arrived, life seemed to speed up. Plans were being made for our impending journey to Ecuador and word was getting out. Our departure was set for September (our baby was due at the end of April). It was really exciting to see the growing interest at our church: the encouragement we had from the former missionaries we knew there was uplifting, and there seemed to be affirmation from everyone.

Unfortunately, my blood pressure became very high again and I had to be admitted to hospital; but this time only for two weeks before the baby was due.

Everything went normally with the birth of our lovely

son, on the 20th April 1967. John was present, and we were thrilled to bits to have a little brother for Mary Jane. I named him Matthew, which means 'Gift of Yahweh'.

The only difficulty was that, inexplicably, my breasts became engorged, which was excruciatingly painful. I got very little sleep and was not coping well. I thought that as soon as I had got over that problem I would be fine – but I wasn't: I then got the dreaded after-baby blues and was very tearful.

The day for my discharge could not come soon enough for me. John had vacated our home while I was in hospital and we were going to be staying with his parents. John had been told he could collect me in the morning, and I was really miserable by the time he turned up around five o'clock that afternoon. He came bustling in, saying: 'I've got to get you to Mum and Dad's quickly as I have a meeting at 7.30.' I was very upset by this, because it was him I really needed.

Once we were in the car, I told him how wretched I was feeling. I burst into tears and sobbed, 'I need you so much, John! I need your comfort and reassurance.' He was distressed to see me in such a state.

Nothing seemed to ease my sense of vulnerability and need. One thing that did help, though, was seeing my little Mary Jane again. She gave me such a welcome, throwing her arms around my neck and saying, 'My mammy! My mammy is back!' Her excitement on seeing her new baby brother was really lovely.

I had hoped that my emotional instability would end but unfortunately it increased. Being with John's parents didn't help. I thought that Mum Hart would understand, but she didn't really. She tried, bless her, but I was left feeling embarrassed that I was so down and needy.

Looking back, I know now that I had a form of post-natal depression. It lasted a couple of months or so.

I would put Matthew in the pram and ask Mum Hart to care for Mary Jane while I went for a walk – she loved our daughter and was always happy to look after her. I would go out of the village and, once I was alone, I would give vent to all the turmoil I felt inside, sobbing my heart out as I asked God to sort me out.

One day, I got home to find John there unexpectedly. He could see I had been crying and he put his arms around me and said, 'What's the matter?' I told him I felt lost, lonely and unloved. 'But I love you, Brenda,' he replied. I said: 'I don't feel your love, John. This awful loneliness surrounds me. I know that the Lord loves me, just as I am; but I don't feel loved.'

John must have confided in his dear friend Victor Jack, because he and his wife invited us to spend our last month in England with them. It was so good for me, and for us as a family. As the weeks went by I recovered my equilibrium, and by the time we set sail for Ecuador I was my normal self.

The church put on an inspiring service to say goodbye to us. The singing was wonderful and the last hymn was 'We rest on Thee, our shield and our defender'. I had many mixed feelings in my heart – huge relief that at last we were on our way, a sense of deep unworthiness, a sense of inadequacy, too, but also of wonder that God could use someone like me and assurance that, as we were being obedient to his calling, he would never leave us or forsake us.

We were sailing from Liverpool in mid September on the cargo ship *El Pizarro*. I was overjoyed to see my father, my sister and brother-in-law with their first baby, and some of my church family from Cutsyke, but of course there was sadness. It wasn't easy to say farewell to loved ones – I had struggled for some years with living so far away from my family and it never got any easier. My lovely dad, who had given his children such wise, down-to-earth love, was now very frail and I knew that with his lung condition he could not live many more years.

He came to see our cabin and when we got down there, he turned to my husband and said: 'John, I know I'm a baby Christian but I would like to give you and Brenda and the babies my blessing.' He got us to kneel and he prayed for us, thanking the Lord for bringing us this far and commending us to his protection and care.

Then he hugged us both and said to me: 'My darling daughter, I will never see your face again. I will be with Jesus when you come back to England.'

He was right, too. He lived just over a year after our parting – my wonderful father, the loveliest dad anybody could ever have had. He knew the Lord for only a year or so and yet he had always seemed like a Christian – a better one than some Christian men I knew! His short life had been full of tragedy but I can't remember any bitterness in him regarding its many hardships, and he was loved and admired in his community.

He will always be my hero, so brave, so forgiving and so very loving. So often he was my champion and he enabled me to be who I am today. I thank my heavenly Father for my dad.

The time came for all visitors to leave the ship. John and I waved everybody goodbye and remained standing on deck with our arms around each other, me holding Matthew and John holding Mary Jane, until the lights of Liverpool were lost in the distance.

To some extent it grieved us both to be separated from so many loved ones. This was a very new experience for John – he hadn't known any other place than East Anglia and he was very bound up in the lives of so many family and friends. I knew instinctively that this would cause him some suffering on the voyage and I silently prayed that the Lord would help him through this – and that I would be sensitive to his needs.

We were not very far out to sea when I began to feel a bit seasick, and I continued to do so for a good few days. I had to make feeds for Matthew below decks, in a space that was quite small and claustrophobic, and sometimes that made the nausea worse. John would tease me about it – he hadn't felt the tiniest bit sick!

I did get my sea legs eventually, though, and after that I never looked back. For a week or so, we had a hurricane chasing us, called 'Brenda' (can you believe it?), and now poor John was laid low – and it wasn't just nausea, he was really sick until the sea became calmer. Poor chap, I was tempted to tease him but I thought: No, he's suffering enough!

There was a swimming pool on board and we got the children in it every day. Matthew was only five months old but by the end of the voyage both of them could swim. All the sailors found it very amusing and would come to watch, it was so cute.

Everyone made a fuss of the little ones and they loved their time on that ship. Mary Jane was thrilled to have Daddy around so much and always preferred to have him do things for her. If it wasn't 'Me do it!', she would say, 'My daddy do it!' – and would emphasise the 'my'.

For me, it was so lovely for us all to be together so much. I realised that John needed space, because (as I had expected) it affected him deeply that he was leaving so much of himself behind; but by the time we got to the Panama Canal he seemed to be much more himself.

He had a camera and he was so excited and full of fun! It made me very glad to see 'Boy John' again. How the memory makes me smile! I had missed that glow of happiness in him for so long – since the birth of Mary Jane there had been a kind of sadness in him, a shadow of something that was not right in his world.

We had one stopover, in Bermuda. We had a really lovely weekend there, and were made to feel so welcome at the church we went to. The service was very exuberant and we loved it.

Our mealtimes were interesting. We ate with the

captain, and he was such a gentleman! (All the officers at least were British, with very British accents.) He delighted to engage Mary Jane in conversation. He told us they rarely had children on board and it was a treat for him to hear her baby talk.

There were other passengers on board: an older couple, who were missionaries going to Brazil on their last assignment, and a young woman who we tried in vain to get to know, as she was very private and self-contained.

The two missionaries – their names escape me – were lovely people and they took quite an interest in us and all we wanted to do in Ecuador. They asked us whether we spoke Spanish and I told them that John had done a beginner's course. I had longed to do it, too, but I couldn't go as there was no one else to care for Mary Jane.

Eventually we arrived at Guayaquil, the port city of Ecuador. Some missionaries were meeting us there and we had to wait, ready to disembark, while everything was being offloaded.

What confusion there was! I was carrying Matthew and my hand luggage only and John was just in front of me, carrying Mary Jane, when some man came running up the gangplank and very roughly tried to grab hold of her. While others ran up to stop him, someone else tried to grab my handbag. It was the most frightening experience.

Two people, obviously missionaries, came to our rescue and quickly bundled us into a car and drove off at speed, with tyres screeching. One of them told us that the port was one of the most dangerous places in the country. We were really scared!

As we were to find out, Ecuadorians really are the most gentle and friendly people, especially towards people of European appearance; and yet there are some who would kill you for your boots. We were to have many such experiences in the years we lived there.

Chapter 9

We stayed for a night in Guayaquil and then took a flight to Quito, the capital city, where we were met by Wilfred Tidmarsh. What a thrill that was for John – he was the very missionary who had pointed at him all those years ago! Naturally, they had been in communication with each other for some months before we set out.

Dr Tidmarsh and his wife put us up for a week or so while we looked for a flat to rent. As we were very unsure where we would actually be working, we didn't buy any furniture and borrowed mattresses and other essentials and 'camped' for the months we were in Quito.

John enrolled at the Central University of Ecuador to study Spanish, and we made plans to go eventually to the eastern rainforest to spend Christmas in the village of Shandia, in the very house that Jim and Betty Elliot had built and lived in. John and I had always thought that our deep desire to have medical training had come from the Lord; we knew that TB was a killer and we felt that this was what we would be working in.

In due course, we flew to Shandia in a Mission Aviation Fellowship plane. What an experience that was – and who should be there to meet us, with some other missionaries, but Dr Tidmarsh? What super fellowship we had while we were there! John went out with some of the other men so that he could see the work they were doing and get a sense of whether we would fit into it. It was very enlightening and we just needed time to think and pray afterwards.

Once we were back in Quito, John got on with his Spanish course and I got back into the routine with the little ones.

One day when I was taking Mary Jane and Matthew to a play area with swings and suchlike, I saw a number of indigenous women with babies on their backs, repairing the roads! I could not believe what I was seeing – it really brought tears to my eyes. I couldn't speak to them but I let them see that I was very concerned for them.

The next day, I filled my biggest pan with chicken soup and I took it to these dear women. I couldn't serve them all at once, as I didn't have the dishes, but wow, were they grateful! Some of their babies had some, too.

The desire to help these women in some way each day remained with me all the time we were in Quito. It was an honour to do so, and we became friends – we couldn't communicate in words but we did in other ways. We had some fun, too: Mary Jane was very taken with their babies and always wanted to hold them. John was always interested to hear what we had been up to while he was at the University.

In his turn, he told us what a rush and crush it was to get there and back, and what he had been able to learn about Spanish. He said that their teacher was very patient. He really liked the language and was very happy with the progress he was making.

Some of the mistakes he made while he was still mastering Spanish had us in stitches. Once, he told us that he had been standing in a crowded bus when it jolted and he fell backwards into the lap of a very pretty young woman. He meant to say '*Perdóneme*' – 'Excuse me' – but what he came out with instead was '*Permiso*': 'May I?' He was so embarrassed!

One thing that made life quite difficult for us was that the water supply to the tank on our roof came on only once a day, in the very early hours of the morning, and one of us had to be on hand to open the valve. To begin with, I was often up anyway, as Matthew was still having some early feeds; but one morning when Matthew didn't wake, I didn't, either, and as a result we got no water that day. We had to buy enough just for drinking and cooking.

After that, we had to start setting the alarm clock. It

meant waiting on the roof until the water arrived, and as this went on for several months until we left Quito, poor John became quite sleep-deprived.

He and I talked at length about how we saw things as regards our future work. We both felt that the project the missionaries in Shandia were doing was fantastic, but we were not convinced that they really needed more workers.

One day, we had a visit from an English missionary called Doreen Villareal. She and her Ecuadorian husband, Abdon, were working on the western side of the Andes, on the way down to the Pacific coast, with the only indigenous tribe in those parts, who are known as *Indios Colorados* after the bright red paste they put in their hair.

Doreen told us that the tribe was decreasing in number because of TB. She and Abdon had been trying to help but they had not made much progress – and now they had to take their two younger children to England to settle them in the boarding school where the two older ones were already. Would we be able to help?

So, we went to stay for a week in Santo Domingo de los Colorados, to see where we could fit in. It soon became clear to us that much of the momentum of the Villareals' work, not only among the Colorados but also now among the *mestizos*, people of mixed race, could be lost if there was no one to keep it up. At the time, the Villareals were the only missionaries in the area.

The great need in Santo Domingo challenged us, and we prayed and shared and looked to the Lord to guide us, and slowly we became convinced that this was where we were to go, to take over the work there. We finally moved to Santo Dom in February 1968.

In those days, what is now Ecuador's fourth most populous city was little more than a shanty town in a big clearing in the rainforest. There were no roads except dirt ones and no cars, and all the houses were made of wood or bamboo with roofs of thatch or tin. There were lots of horses everywhere and so, as it was the rainy season, there was mud in abundance!

The bus we travelled on stopped in the centre of town, in a circular plaza surrounded by shops. In the middle of this stood a monumental statue of a Colorado man, which had been put up as a kind of sop to these people because the settlers were cutting down some of the forest that was their home.

The Villareals had bought a large tract of land about 20 minutes' walk away, on which they had built a wooden house for themselves and, a short distance from it, a little bamboo church with a thatched roof.

A small breeze-block clinic was under construction next-door to them and they had hoped we could live in this pro tem until they left for England, when we could move into their home. However, the clinic was not yet completed, as there was a shortage of cement locally, and so instead we had to stay in a typical Colorado house – fully furnished with hammocks.

What fun we had with these – it was hilarious! The children loved them and so did we after a time, but they took some getting used to. When there are two of you in a hammock, you have to be careful you don't knock your partner out of it!

We stayed in that house for the whole of March, though of course we had our meals with Doreen and Abdon until they left. They introduced us to the chief and some other Colorado men – of course, we didn't know their language, so we all spoke in pidgin Spanish.

Many people, when they think of the indigenous people of Ecuador, picture the Quechua of the high Andes, in their trilby hats and ponchos. However, the country has many different tribes, each with their own language, customs – and dress. In those days the Colorados didn't wear many clothes, and the women were bare-breasted.

I found someone to help me learn Spanish, and after Doreen and Abdon had gone I took on their domestic helper, whose name was Elvia. She proved to be worth her weight in gold!

People were coming to see us for spiritual, medical or even legal advice – the very poor *mestizos* and, in large numbers on market days, the Colorados – and I needed someone who could take care of the children if necessary, as well as showing me how to do other things. Moreover, although she was uneducated herself, Elvia could correct me when I pronounced something wrong.

(Mary Jane, too, started to correct me, she was picking the language up so quickly. 'You don't say it like that, Mammy. It's like *this*.' She was so comical!)

Our family life, which my lovely husband had missed before, became such a joy to him. Sometimes, coming into the house after doing a job or seeing someone, he would catch me round the waist and swing me around and dance with me, laughing heartily. We were very, very happy with the way things were working out. Once more, we were serving the Lord shoulder to shoulder and our joy knew no bounds. I had my John back fully.

It took work to win the Colorados over. We helped them in any way we could – John ended up giving injections to their pigs, while I went to assist with a difficult birth just a few months after we arrived. The girl concerned, who was still a child really, lived some distance away – I had to get there by truck and then walk into the forest. It was not exactly an emergency but she was very frightened and I made a hit that day with her and her whole family.

When it was time for me to go, there was a whole crowd who wanted to accompany me back to the road. The Colorados laugh a lot and how they laughed when we came to a deepish stream and I had to shuffle across the plank bridge on my bottom! (I always lost my balance when I tried to walk over such bridges and, to my great embarrassment, I often fell in.)

The rains were expected to stop in April or May, so we decided to visit the few Christians in the immediate area. Most of those who were not members of Abdon's family were recent converts, but they were keen and John began to involve them in our services. Those who could read would do the Bible readings, while others would pray or sing, give a testimony or just help with the refreshments.

John's Spanish was coming on very well and he was doing some speaking. He used visual aids a lot, including fuzzy felt, as he tried hard not to make anyone who was uneducated feel inferior.

Whenever possible, we would point out the thatched church to the people who came to the clinic. Very slowly, our gatherings there began to grow. It was really exciting to be by John's side in all that was happening.

My Spanish teacher was a schoolteacher from the town, called Susie. I managed to interest her in coming to church – we had been having some good talks about the Lord – and slowly she and her husband came to listen to John.

I had decided that I needed to make friends with local people, so I asked Elvia to initiate me into washing our clothes in the river, as so many of our neighbours did. She and I would do it with our babies tied on our backs, while Mary Jane played with the other children at the water's edge. It was great fun! I made so many friends quite quickly and soon some began to come to the services.

My babies were such a novelty – people had never seen little ones with such blond hair and blue eyes! Mary Jane's hair was golden, quite straight and unruly but a beautiful colour. Matthew still had very little hair and he looked a bit like Winston Churchill.

John held a children's evangelistic week and many of the local children came. It was a real success. We started a Sunday school and some of the original members of the church were trained up as teachers, which was a blessing to them as they studied the Bible and grew in their faith, too.

In late May, I developed a skin rash all over me, which looked a bit like measles but wasn't. I felt OK except that I was very tired at times, but I put that down to my very full life.

John was very concerned, however, and decided that we had better take a trip to Quito to have me checked out thoroughly at the HCJB mission hospital. We left the children in Elvia's very safe hands and made an early start on the first bus to leave the central plaza.

(The hospital had been founded in 1955 by the world's first missionary radio station, HCJB, 'the Voice of the Andes', whose call letters stood for 'Heralding Christ Jesus' Blessings' or, in Spanish, '*Hoy Cristo Jesús Bendice*' ['Today Christ Jesus Blesses'].)

The doctor asked me about my periods and I told him that the last three had been quite light but that, what with the heat and being so busy, I had lost quite a lot of weight and I thought that was the reason.

He examined me and said: 'You're pregnant.' What a shock that was! He told me that I must have conceived in March and would be having another Christmas baby. The skin problem was not serious and he would give me some lotion for it.

John had gone to see our lawyer about something while I was with the doctor, but he was waiting for me when I left the consulting room. I told him the news and his reaction was almost disbelief. 'Wow!', he said – and blamed the hammock. 'Come here, my love,' he added, giving me a big hug. 'We'll be in this together. This little one is God's plan for us, he will see us through.'

This time my pregnancy was to be trouble-free, except that the heat caused me some discomfort later on.

The medical work was progressing. In due course, we started immunising the Colorados, which brought ever more people to our clinic. I was seeing lots of babies who were suffering from malnutrition, mainly because their mothers' milk had dried up and they were being fed on watered-down Quaker Oats.

I taught the mothers how to make custard from corn starch, egg yolk, cow's milk and just the tiniest bit of sugar, and told them to come back to see me each week. The babies got much better quite quickly (and this created more contacts, too, for our booming church).

I also started a mother-and-baby health programme, teaching hygiene and nutrition, which was such a help to so many.

As I prepared for the arrival of the new baby, I managed to buy some baby clothes second-hand from some other missionaries, and it was arranged that a colleague of theirs who was coming to Santo Dom for a meeting would bring them with him on the bus. Sadly, he put the package on the luggage rack and then fell asleep. When he woke up, he found to his consternation that it had been stolen.

How distressed he was when he told us! Naturally we were unhappy, but we couldn't tell him that we were very low on funds and it was going to be a real challenge to replace everything.

However, our wonderful Lord had it all in hand. The man told his family and his friends what had happened – and the baby clothes they brought to his house as gifts would eventually fill a big drum! It was an enormous surprise when this was delivered to us in late October.

After I had taken what I was going to need, I was able to help many of the very disadvantaged mothers where we lived. What an encouragement that was for us! The Lord never fails his children.

Although my pregnancy was problem-free, John wanted me to be checked out at the mission hospital in Quito every six weeks. I remained in Santo Dom until the third week of November, but we felt it would be best if I and the children stayed in the capital for the last few weeks and John then joined us a week before I gave birth.

We were renting a room in Quito from a missionary there named John Munday and we often stayed there when we had to be in the capital. It wasn't fully furnished, but we had put some mattresses on the floor and we made do with what else there was.

I had Elvia with me and she looked after the children in the mornings, as I had signed up for some Spanish classes to iron out some of my grammatical confusion. The classes helped me a lot, though to this day I still have difficulties with some of the trickier bits of grammar.

The teacher was very amused at my Spanish – I spoke with the coastal accent and used a lot of colloquial expressions. I told her quite shyly that I knew my Spanish was bad and she said: 'Oh no, you have good Spanish of the area – you communicate well. Let's just say that you don't "speak the Queen's Spanish", as in "the Queen's English".'

That really got me laughing – I don't speak that, either!

The only picture there is of me, Marlene and Maurice as children

The blushing groom and his bride

Above: We were thrilled to have a little brother for Mary Jane –
but I was also unmistakably anxious and unhappy.
Below: Quito, 1967. John loved the view of the mountains from our roof.

Above: If only this image could be in colour! Young Colorado lads
in the late Sixties
Below: Mary Jane just had to tell her friends about AnaMari's arrival,
but Matthew was very put out.

Above: Despite my grin, back in England I felt very sad and lonely.
Below: Life on furlough in the depths of the countryside
was not exactly luxurious!

Above: In 1974, in rehab after my cardiac arrest, I helped with light nursing duties at Papworth Hospital.
Below: With Mary Jane and Matthew on the beach at Atacames

Clockwise from left: Matthew in 1974 and AnaMari and Mary Jane in '75

Above: Matthew, Mary Jane and AnaMari dressed for 'physical jerks'
Below: On holiday in Atacames with (left to right) Angelita, Brendita,
Mary Jane, Tinie, Matthew, Vivvie and AnaMari. The woman
with her face half hidden is a visiting missionary.

Chapter 10

Everything went to plan: John joined us and I started labour the night of the 18th December. With Elvia there to look after the children, it was about five or six in the morning when we set out for the hospital.

Once I was checked in, I had to wait to be examined. I knew I was getting quite close to having the baby and after a while I became a bit agitated at the delay. 'I need to be seen quickly,' I said to John. 'Go and find a doctor or a nurse!' He seemed to be gone a long time, but eventually a doctor came and took me and John into a delivery room. He told me I had a long way to go yet. 'Please don't go!', I pleaded. 'I'm about to have my baby.' He patted me and promised to come back soon.

I said: 'John, put the delivery table up, please! He's wrong, I know it.' John was a bit doubtful that I might be right, not the doctor, so he just stood there. I seized his arm and in a panicky voice commanded: 'Do as I say!' So he did. I asked him to look and see if he could see the baby's head, and indeed he could.

He was about to set off to find the doctor but my pains were such that I knew I was about to give birth. I shouted, 'Please, John, stay!' and he came to his senses and assisted – and within a few minutes AnaMari arrived in his hands.

After he had reassured me that all was well, he laid the baby on the table and went to find the doctor, who returned, very shamefaced, to cut the cord and deliver the placenta. I held my new little daughter for a while, and then a nurse took her away to allow me to get some rest. I was taken to a bed in a double room. All I wanted was to sleep, and that's what I did.

I was woken up by a loud yell. Someone was in distress. I realised that it was the woman I was sharing my room with, so I got up and, going over to her, asked: 'Are you giving birth?' She nodded her head frantically as she weathered another strong pain, and then began yelling loudly. I looked for a bell but couldn't find one.

I knew it must be dinner time – I could smell food cooking. I looked in the corridor but there was no one to be seen. The poor woman was now screaming, so I went back to her and said, 'Look, I'm a nurse and I can help you. Don't scream or shout, just use your pain to push!' – and after several good pushes her baby boy was born.

I went out into the corridor again – still nobody. I walked along it and eventually found a domestic, so I sent her to summon help and then I went back to comfort the woman as she lay shivering from all the fear and stress. I wrapped her and the baby up as well as I could, and stayed beside her until someone arrived.

How pleased I was to get back into bed then! I had had only three hours' sleep.

The doctor who had been responsible for my care said to a nurse friend of mine: 'I don't know how I'm going to face Mrs Hart when she comes for her six-weeks check!' He did have the grace to apologise when I did.

How thrilled Mary Jane was to have a new baby in the house! AnaMari was a real joy for her, but Matthew was not so keen – whenever I was nursing her, he would want to be on my knee, too. He was a year and eight months old and still very much a baby.

He was rather shy and always wanted to have me in his field of view. He was also slow in his talking and almost everything else in comparison with how Mary Jane had developed – he couldn't say his sisters' names, so he called them 'JJ' and 'Awie'.

(AnaMari was half-named after John's mother, Hannah – the H would not be sounded in Ecuador. As teenagers, both she and Mary Jane would drop the second half of their name, but even today I still pray for them by the full names I gave them.)

To start with, everything went well as we got into the

swing of having another newborn in the household. I even strapped her to my back when I was doing the washing in the river. How my neighbours laughed and cheered when Elvia and I arrived with three children! *'Que valiente gringuita!'* ('What a brave little foreigner!') they would cry out. They really took to me – and a good few started coming to church.

I'm not sure whether Bruce and Joyce Moore had arrived before or after Christmas 1968, but they were two people I shall never forget. What very dear friends they would prove to be to us all the years we knew them! They became so involved in our lives, for as long as we were in Ecuador, and made a real impact for good on us as a family. Joyce not only encouraged me, she helped me in so many different ways.

They were linguists with Wycliffe Bible Translators and had been living in one of the Colorado communities for about 10 years, I think, working to put their language, known as Tsafiki, into written form. It was a very complex task, analysing a language that uses sounds not found in other languages and devising an alphabet to represent them, and so it was quite a slow process.

They had four children, three of them studying at an American academy in Quito and the fourth, a younger daughter called Carol, living with them in Santo Dom. Beckie, who was a teenager, came down in the holidays. They had all just returned from the States, where they had been on 'home assignment'. Their plan was to build a wooden house next to the Villareals' house, where we were staying.

How pleased and excited we were to have such super neighbours! They came to our little church, and Beckie and Carol in particular loved our children and sometimes played with them. Later, they would sometimes help with Mary Jane's education.

One day, John called into the local hospital to offer to give blood (his blood group was O negative, which meant that anyone could receive it). We had been subject to some rather nasty prejudice on the local radio, as the Catholics in the area regarded us as heretics and had been trying to make people afraid of us. The hospital was run by nuns, so it was (to say the least) quite bold of him to go there; but actually it was a great opportunity to show ourselves to them.

John was very respectful and told them: 'I realise that you think we are against you, but we want to help your people just as you are doing. Please let us be of service!' He gave them our phone number and left it at that.

It wasn't long before they called him in, and that was the start of our good relations with the local Catholics. Some of the nuns were teachers and later, when John was showing the Fact and Faith films in the town, that became a way into their schools, too.

The work we were involved in was growing all the time and we were increasingly accepted in the town. More and more people were coming to our little church each week and John and some of the other men decided to extend it, which early in 1969 they did.

Our teaching had to meet the needs of people who had very little knowledge of the Bible and Bruce assisted with some of it, for which John and I were very grateful. He and Joyce were so helpful and encouraging, although most of their work was with the Colorados and so they were very busy in one of their settlements 'in the sticks'.

Bruce told John, 'I can hardly believe you've only been speaking Spanish just over a year. You have an excellent command of the language when you teach, and I'm impressed with the messages you're giving, which are clear and interesting and informative.'

John decided that once the rainy season was over, in late April or early May, we would have a 'tent campaign'.

From HCJB, he invited an evangelist, some singers and an artist who illustrated the talks as they went along in fluorescent chalk. The tent was quite a large one and when the day arrived to erect it, it was all hands on deck. I can still see my darling Mary Jane, so tiny and sweet, looking thrilled by all the buzz and calling out to John: '*Cuídese, papito lindo!*' ('Take care, lovely Daddy!'). How everyone loved her, and loved to hear her talk! (She really was a good talker, and always has been.)

Once the tent was up, we all had something to drink and relaxed for a while, talking about the team that was arriving the next day. They had been booked into the best hotel in town for four nights – the campaign was going to be three full days – because we didn't want anyone to get sick.

We were all feeling excited, not to say rather pleased with ourselves, when it started to rain. We looked up in disbelief. And did it rain! Wow, it was just like the rainy season!

I and some of the other women dashed into our house to pray while the men worked like crazy bailing the water out of the now sagging canvas. Eventually, after two hours or more, the rain stopped. The men were exhausted but, praise the Lord, they had saved the tent.

We had the most amazing campaign. The evangelistic team did a magnificent job and the whole event left us exhilarated and encouraged for weeks.

One of the difficulties this amazing blessing presented was the follow-up of so many new Christians. We had never had to deal with so many illiterate people before. We encouraged people to learn to read and organised classes, but it was not easy. We didn't have enough teachers and some students found the lessons too hard and time-consuming, and as a result some never did learn to read. However, they gained a lot from the lovely songs we sang in our services, which got some doctrine into their minds and hearts set to music, as it were.

So many people had come to the Lord that we were now once again very squashed for space in our church.

That year, we had no mail for six months or so – as I recall it, there was a prolonged strike in England that disrupted the post. At any event, our funds didn't reach us, and this, as well as not receiving any letters, made us feel very isolated. Life became very lean and it really tested our faith.

One day, I remember, we all but ran out of food. We had some cereal and bananas to give the little ones for breakfast, but John and I didn't eat, we were so concerned for our children. We sat at the table and John said: 'Let's thank the Lord for what he will provide! He won't let us down.' So, we did just that.

We were holding hands as he prayed and I squeezed John's hand and we looked into each other's eyes. We felt so close to each other – but it was God's wonderful presence we felt the most.

It was no more than five minutes later that there was a loud knock on the door. I went to see who it was, and there stood a man we knew, a very new Christian called Don César. He was a *mestizo* working for the Colorados as a labourer out in the forest and he must have come a long way to call on us.

My eyes nearly popped out of my head when I saw him: he was holding a large 'head' of plantain – for our family, at least three or four weeks' supply! He also had a net bag full of eggs hanging round his neck.

'Come in!', I cried. 'What brings you here at this hour?' He proceeded to tell us that God had woken him early and told him that the missionaries with the babies were in need of some food. 'So, here I am with supplies for you,' he concluded.

John and I were astonished at what he told us. We were so humbled, and our tears flowed in thanks for this obvious miracle. When we told Don César our situation, he cried, too. 'To think', he said, 'that almighty God has used someone like me this day. It is the most wonderful thing.'

He never could learn to read, but he was someone that God was to use time and time again. He was such a delightful man in every way, and very committed to his Lord and Saviour.

During that time of scarcity, AnaMari fell sick. She was four months old and it was difficult to know what to do because we couldn't tell what was wrong with her. I tried different medicines to no avail, and spent many nights pacing the floor. We couldn't afford to go to Quito to consult a doctor (and anyway I was concerned about the effect the altitude would have on such a small baby), so we prayed continually for her healing.

In the middle of one night, I was beside myself with anxiety and sorrow as my little one, who had been screaming in pain, seemed to faint, her eyes rolling up in her head. I cried to John, 'She's dying! My baby's dying!'

He took her in his arms and cuddled her, and with a faltering voice prayed: 'This little one is yours, Lord. Her life is in your hands. Help us in this trial!'

Well, AnaMari slowly started to come round. After a while, she seemed much calmer and less distressed, so I tried to feed her and, wonder of wonders, she settled and fell into an untroubled sleep.

John and I were both still shaking from the ordeal we had just gone through. I felt stunned but full of gratitude, and I could see that in his own way John, too, was processing his emotions. We held each other tight and quietly said 'Thank you, Lord!' over and over again. We were both reduced to tears by the awe we felt.

AnaMari didn't look back after that but continued to thrive. John joked that she was God's *yappa* to us. In the market, when a regular customer has made a substantial purchase, a trader will say, 'Here is a *yappa*,' holding out a bunch of grapes or suchlike as a gift.

AnaMari has always been something special to us as a family. Mary Jane and Matthew have always loved her, protected her and championed her.

The other distressing experience we had at this time was getting the news – delayed by the postal strike – that my father had died in February. My grief was intense and very, very painful. My heart was broken for a while. At the same time, it didn't seem real – I hadn't been able to mourn with my family at his funeral and I felt very alone. In time, I was able to accept his loss and rejoice that he was now with the Lord, which was far better. At last, my lovely dad was at peace and praising his Saviour in heaven. One day, I shall see him again.

In 1972, I went to see his grave in Yorkshire when I was on home leave and it was good to pay my respects to his memory and once more thank the Lord for my father.

One day, we had a visit from a doctor from the mission hospital in Quito. They wanted to promote women's health, especially among the poor in towns like Santo Dom, and Dr John had heard about us and heard that we were nurses. He wanted to know whether we knew anything about family planning. Well, we didn't know much at all – in fact, we didn't use anything ourselves!

He enlisted us all the same and over a succession of many visits he showed us what had to be done. He was about to go back to America on home assignment, so he left us all his equipment and taught John to fit the coil. (In our area, where very few people could read, no other form of contraception was ever considered.) The insertion of the coil was regarded as man's work, and my husband proved to be a dab hand at it!

Thus, we got not just an education but an introduction to the culture of the Sixties at its very end, which made us smile. It was a real blessing to us as a couple. I was fitted with the coil myself and it brought such freedom and joy into our lives, as into the lives of so many others. At that time, no one could foresee the downside of so much freedom, how easily we humans turn a blessing into a curse...

Our clinic became one of the first few family-planning clinics in Ecuador. It was an eye-opener for us as we learnt more of the tragic lives of so many of the women of that area. Some had had as many as 20 pregnancies by their late twenties or thirties. Families were very large, though the infant-mortality rate was horrific; many children were very malnourished, and some had rickets. Their mothers were very thin and had lost many of their teeth, which made them look like old women.

I have a vivid memory of John and me, after one particularly disheartening day seeing so much misery, holding each other in bed and weeping over all the suffering we were witnessing. We took it all to Jesus, the 'man of sorrows acquainted with grief', and asked him to strengthen us and fill us with compassion for so many vulnerable people.

This ministry was to be another way in which our church family would grow. John must have improved the lives of thousands of women and children in this practical way; but our greatest desire was that they should find the Saviour. We had a captive audience at the clinic every day as people waited their turn, so we preached the gospel to them. We also invited many of our new Christians to give their testimony, which helped to build up both them and the church.

Chapter 11

In the second half of 1969, one of the members of the church told John that he was going to sell some land. We knew that the Villareals were coming back soon and that we would need rehousing, and we thought that maybe we could have our own place.

However, the land in question was five miles out of town, on the main road to Quito, which made me a bit worried about my continued involvement in the work. How would I manage the children and everything? Travelling backwards and forwards with the little ones would be difficult, Mary Jane was coming up to five years old and I needed to start teaching her some basics.

We pondered and prayed and decided nonetheless to purchase the land and build a wooden house on it. It was quite a large tract, with trees and a little river, and it really seemed ideal for us. We took Bruce and Joyce to see it; they thought it was a lovely setting and encouraged us to buy it.

We didn't have all the necessary funds to begin with, but we were allowed to pay in instalments and once we had made the first payment we were able to start building.

We had a very dear Christian friend called Fausto, who was an amazing character. He had been born with a hole in his heart and John had been giving him medical help. Fausto was a carpenter and so was well able to construct a wooden house.

He had previously lived in the high Andes with his father and his family, and they had all become Christians long before they moved to Santo Dom. After they found the Lord, the whole family had been cruelly treated by the local kind of Roman Catholics – they were often beaten and humiliated publicly, but they remained true to their faith.

They had sold up their farm and moved to Santo Dom,

some time before we did, after hearing about this new town from a relative. For a long time they had worshipped as a house church, but once they heard about our services they joined us, and they became very useful and valued members of our fellowship.

Fausto started making plans for the house with us around November. He told us that he wouldn't start building until the rainy season was over but in the meantime he would apply himself to clearing the land and marking out where we wanted the house to go.

Abdon and Doreen were supposed to be coming back in early 1970 but we didn't have a firm date. They hadn't intended to be away so long, but their older son and daughter had been having problems, so they stayed on. John and I would probably need to rent somewhere if our house was not ready when they returned.

One piece of good news we had from the Villareals was that they had been given some funds to build a lovely new circular breeze-block church. They had some land set aside which they were donating for the purpose. The new church was to be called El Buen Pastor ('The Good Shepherd').

Just after the start of the rainy season, we heard that there had been an outbreak of polio in Santo Dom, although we had not actually seen any cases and so we wondered whether it was true.

One day, a young man turned up carrying his seven-year-old son, who was obviously infected. The boy was very thin and couldn't walk. The father, who was called Marcus, was in tears as he said that he hoped we could cure his son, José. We had to admit that we had no way of doing so, but we told him about the Lord and how he can, and sometimes does, heal people miraculously. We invited him to put his trust in the will of God for José.

We prayed with him and simply asked the Lord Jesus

that José would become well again and that he and his father would come to know him as their Saviour.

A few days later, Marcus and José walked into our house, huge smiles on their faces. 'Jesus has done it!', Marcus cried. 'He has healed my son!' He accepted the Saviour that very day, and has been a vibrant Christian ever since.

José accepted the Lord as well a couple of years later. Once when we met them both, John said to him: 'You still have that limp. We thought it would get better.' 'Yes,' said José, 'but I'm glad that it's still with me, because it does not let me forget how Jesus worked a miracle. It also gives me the opportunity to tell others about him and his wonderful love.'

Just before Christmas, we had a visit from John Munday, the missionary in Quito whose room we were renting there. I was down by the river washing clothes when he arrived with a party of Canadians who were making a study of missionary work in Latin America.

Elvia, who had returned to the house to start preparing dinner, brought them down to meet me, which was a lovely surprise. After they had helped me get the children and the laundry back to the house, I served them some drinks and they plied me with questions about our work and the growth of our church. They didn't stay long, but it cheered me greatly to be able to converse in my own language.

A few weeks later, John Munday turned up again in a van, in which he had brought me a washing machine. It was huge, almost like a piece of industrial equipment. It had a motor on the outside, and some big rollers to squeeze the clothes dry. I was flabbergasted! He said: 'The Canadians thought this might make your life easier.'

Apparently, some missionaries in the capital were going back to the States and were selling off all their stuff, and when the group heard that this included a washing machine they all thought of me. How wonderfully kind of my Lord to provide such an amazing piece of equipment!

It took me a week or more to get the hang of the beast; but once I did, it was marvellous – and especially the rollers: my washing was dry in no time at all.

It was a great Christmas that year. Bruce and Joyce and their family were with us, our two girls had their fifth and first birthdays and the Lord was blessing us all in so many ways. We celebrated communion together, sang and praised our wonderful Lord – what a fantastic time we had!

Joyce was a very good musician: she played both the piano and the piano accordion, and had a beautiful singing voice, too. When they were able to join us in church, the singing and worship time was amazing.

Fausto the carpenter was a wonderful friend to us. He was still quite young – something like 21 or 22, I think; he was single and didn't appear to have a girlfriend. He was a very intelligent man and a real student of God's word and could preach well. He loved getting out to outlying places that the gospel had not yet reached, and he and John would go on evangelistic trips out into the rainforest, where small family groups lived.

These people were mainly uneducated *mestizos* who lived off the land around them. A number of these families came to know the Lord and they would make the long trek every Sunday to get to church in Santo Dom. What dear, humble people they were, their love of the Lord so childlike and practical! We often had the most amazing eggs from them, huge with double yolks.

After one of these evangelistic excursions, John became quite unwell – he had a fever and all his joints were swollen painfully. We took him to the mission hospital in Quito to be examined, and they told us he had been infected with something (the name escapes me) by a rat. He recalled that he and Fausto had seen a rat when they had been sleeping in an outhouse on one of their trips. With the treatment he was given, John recovered fully – but it was awful while it lasted.

Lots of things had changed in Santo Dom over the last two years. An actual road had been built from the centre of the plaza almost to the Villareals' house. Some of the wooden dwellings were being rebuilt with breeze blocks, as were the shops in the central plaza. The monumental statue of the Colorado man was restored and repainted.

We began to shop at a store named Bombolí and we made this a family time – we would make our purchases and then have some food there. Our children always wanted *maduros* (fried plantain) and egg.

The next big event locally was the construction of a huge stadium called the Coliseo. There were always children on the streets and a lot of the boys worked shining shoes. We made friends with them and invited them to come to church. Little Mary Jane was very popular with them; once a week, she and her daddy would have their shoes cleaned and the boys would always pretend to fight to do hers.

There was an unwritten rule that whenever you ate at Bombolí you left some food on your plate so that one of the shoeshine boys could have it. Mary Jane and Matthew would try to make sure that the same boy got their leftovers each week, and if that little fellow was not around they would be quite concerned. 'Will he have any dinner today, Mammy?', they would ask.

We were always made a fuss of at Bombolí, and if ever we were in financial difficulties the owner told John that, if need be, we could run up a bill and pay when we had the money. If I remember correctly, that happened only twice.

The building work began on our house in April, and it was such fun occasionally to go and see the progress they were making. The house was to be on stilts, which left a large and very useful working area underneath it. It was very simple and functional, with mesh windows and a tin roof. There were four bedrooms and an open-plan living area which would serve as a kitchen, a dining room and a sitting room. The bathroom and toilet were under the house.

It was well away from the main road – Fausto and the other men he had helping him constructed a long drive – and it was so very beautiful, with many lovely trees. All you could hear was the sound of the little river flowing by.

When we finally moved in, however, it was quite traumatic. John had arranged for someone to look after the Villareals' house the night before we moved out, while we all waited in the new house. Everything was packed up, ready for the next day.

When John went down with the truck we had hired to collect all our stuff, he found to his horror that the house had been emptied. We were left without clothes, bedding, household linen and many other things we had bought in Ecuador – kitchen utensils, musical instruments, books and toys and oh, so much more! (Fortunately, they missed the washing machine, which we kept outside the house under a big tarpaulin...)

How we managed to replace everything, bit by bit, I don't remember. Their theft was hard to take in, but we recovered our spirits quite quickly.

We named our new home 'Buckingham Palace' for a joke and put a sign to that effect on the gate. One day, when John was out, I saw a very posh car turn off the Quito road onto our drive. I ran down to meet it and as I got near, a man in the passenger seat wound down his window and asked: 'Who lives here?'

I replied: 'My name is Brenda Hart and my husband and I are missionaries from England.' With a big grin, he said: 'So, you're the Queen of Harts?'

It turned out that he was the British ambassador, so I invited him and his driver in for tea. When we were all settled, I introduced my children. I explained who the gentlemen were, and Mary Jane asked the ambassador: 'How is the Queen?'

The two men were so nice and gave the three children a lot of attention. The ambassador, whose name was Peter Mennell, wanted to know what we were doing in Ecuador and when I told him about our church work and the health work we were involved in, he seemed very interested. When they left, he made me promise that when John and I were next in Quito we would call at the consulate and arrange a time to have tea with him.

Which we did, more than once. Peter was such a good friend to us!

Chapter 12

El Buen Pastor was still going forward. It was organised largely according to Brethren principles, with elders and deacons – we had a definite team ministry – although naturally some things were different.

The next big development for us was the amazing gift of a Land Rover, which really revolutionised our lives. Victor Jack, our dear friend from Bury St Eds, had organised this and led the fundraising for it.

John asked a well-known Latin American evangelist (who I think was called Santiago Garabia) to lead a Billy Graham-style campaign in the magnificent new Coliseo. All the Christians in Santo Dom were invited to be a part of this venture, and it really brought all the evangelicals together.

It involved a lot of hard work before, during and even after the event, as we pulled out all the stops. Many people came to the Lord and all the evangelical churches grew.

I'm not sure when John started doing programmes on the local radio station. I think it had been early in 1970 that someone told the owners about him and they got in touch. What an amazing opportunity for the evangelical church to have! The first series he did was on marriage, the family and morality and we were astounded by how much good feedback his teaching got. Years later, they broadcast those recordings again.

In May, about a month after the campaign in the Coliseo, I began to feel unwell, with a bone-aching tiredness that I could not shake off. Fortunately, Dr John from HCJB was coming to Santo Dom to discuss the family-planning clinic with John and he was able to give me a thorough examination. He told me that my liver was very swollen and he was convinced I had amoebic hepatitis.

The good news, he said, was that it wasn't contagious;

the bad news was that I would have to have complete bed rest, not even being allowed to sit up. In that event, my liver could and would renew itself – but it would mean that John had to look after me well.

He took a stool specimen and a blood sample for examination in Quito and the results confirmed his diagnosis. As a result, I was flat in bed for six weeks.

One consequence of this was that, after two weeks, John decided that we should have a fortnight's holiday at Atacames on the coast. It would be easy to make me up a bed in the back of the new Land Rover and we would take Elvia and do the journey as slowly as necessary.

John made that holiday so wonderful, and how the children loved the sand and the sea! By the end of it I was beginning to feel much better, and I think it did John a lot of good, too. He still had a tendency to push himself too hard and had needed that break just as much as I did.

When Dr John came again to examine me, he told me: 'You've done well! Your liver is now normal size, so it's time for you to start very slowly to mobilise, just a little more each week until I see you again in a month's time.'

Praise the Lord, I recovered well! By August, I was engaging again in all our activities.

The Villareals returned at last, which meant more hands on deck. They were active with us in the main church work but were also, like the Moores, very involved with the Colorados. We did some work with the Colorados, too, but mainly on the medical front.

It was about this time that we heard that a young couple from Suffolk called David and Rita Butcher were coming out to Santo Dom as missionaries. We knew them a little, but not well. It was late 1970 or early 1971 when they arrived. Fausto put up an extra wooden house on our land which they were going to use until they knew what they would be doing.

We were so pleased when they chose to join us where

we were. The first imperative for them was to learn the language. They also needed time to settle in and to get used to the heat and the different food.

David found Spanish a bit easier than Rita. It was really hard for the women, because they didn't have the freedom the men had to go out on their own and mix with people. It is constantly hearing the language spoken and having to use as much as you know to respond to people that slowly builds up confidence, which is so important.

A few weeks after they arrived, they gave us the most amazing news: Rita was pregnant! It had been a long trip from England by boat, and that is how their lovely daughter, Amanda, came into being...

How special it was for all of us to get together! There were more missionaries in the area than had ever been known before. Abdon and Doreen, Bruce and Joyce, David and Rita, John and me, plus the Moore children when they were around, and of course our little ones, too. We had so many lovely times together – all in English!

I had started to do play school with Mary Jane, and I hoped in the future to teach her with the aid of a correspondence course (which I did eventually).

The church services were really joyous and exuberant. There was a sensitivity developing with more prayerful songs, especially when celebrating communion, as we followed the Holy Spirit's leading. There were more and more young people at the church, especially in their mid teens and twenties. Some were musical, playing the guitar or maracas and other such instruments of rhythm.

Members of the youth group would sometimes come to visit us in the school holidays, in pairs or even alone. One girl, named Guisela, came quite often on her own. I didn't know her quite as well as the others but she seemed to love playing with our children. The only problem was that she would turn up when John and I had planned some family time, so we had to kind of include her.

My involvement in town was somewhat reduced as

Elvia was pregnant and so I couldn't leave the children to her in the way I had been able to before. We found out that she had a younger sister, Gladis, who was rather keen to work for us. We got her to join us before Elvia left us so that she would know what was expected of her. She proved to be every bit as good as her sister.

John's activity on all fronts grew ever more hectic, which concerned the other missionaries. On one occasion, he upset me deeply. There was a fiesta on over the weekend and I said: 'Let's go and see what's happening in town!' He was already going himself, but I longed to be there with him, too. 'That wouldn't be good for the little ones,' he replied. I suggested that maybe we could take Mary Jane but leave Matthew and AnaMari with Gladis. 'No way!', he replied. 'They're not that used to her.'

He proposed that he should come back about two in the afternoon and we would then all go out to the new swimming pool in the town and then have a picnic. I thought this was a great idea – this pool was the latest sensation locally – and the children were very excited. 'Daddy is taking us swimming in the new pool!', cried Mary Jane, jumping about and clapping her hands.

That morning, we did a bit of schoolwork, finished all our chores and had some lunch. Gladis and I prepared the picnic with the help of the children and we were all ready to go. When two o'clock came and went, I was very concerned. The sad fact is that John didn't show up.

The two older children were in tears, so we had our picnic near our little river, Gladis taught the children a game she used to play as a little girl and I read them one of their favourite stories. I was very worried. What could have happened to John? Had he had an accident? Had he been attacked?

The children were ready for bed when he turned up, so I said (brightly, but not feeling so): 'Maybe Daddy will tuck you in tonight.' As he was doing so, I heard Mary

Jane say: 'You're a very naughty daddy. You promised to be with us.'

Later, I said to a shamefaced John: 'You'd better have a very good reason for what happened today!'

He told me he had met some of the youth group and they had all gone to watch the parade and then they had eaten. Some of them needed lifts home, so he took them. A few of them lived further out of town and he thought he would have time to take them as well, but it was an area he didn't know and by the time he had dropped off the last one it was dark – and then he got hopelessly lost and it took him ages to find his way home.

I sat there not knowing what to say. I was so unhappy that he had put a crowd of young people before the children and me.

After breakfast the next day, once the children were playing happily, I asked Gladis to keep an eye on them while John and I went down to the river. At least we would be more private there.

Feeling heavy-hearted and quite angry, I told him: 'Your behaviour yesterday disappointed me deeply. It was bad enough for me, but you made a promise to your children, too. They should have been your first priority as soon as you had all eaten.'

He shrugged his shoulders and we stood there in silence for quite a while. He didn't see that he had acted wrongly, which made me very resentful. I was reminded of how I had suffered after Mary Jane was born – and my heart was now full of anger as well as pain. I was so choked up, but I was determined not to cry. It was evident that he wasn't going to say anything, so I started walking back to the house.

John stayed by the river for some time. Then he came to the house and said that he had to be in town, and off he went.

As soon as I had an opportunity, I had a heart-to-heart with my dear friend Joyce. I wept as I told her of the pain of the past, and (as we were due for furlough soon) my fear for the future.

On one of his evangelistic trips with Fausto, John got covered in insect bites from his ankles to his knees. Unfortunately, they got very infected, and some of the bites on his calves actually became quite ulcerous, which worried me. What made the problem worse was that he couldn't see that he needed to give his legs a rest.

Bruce and Joyce were quite concerned about John's workload and one day, when for once I had managed to get him to have a lie-down, Bruce turned up, quite out of the blue, and said that he needed to talk to us both.

He explained that Joyce had told him what had happened on the day of the fiesta. 'Now,' he went on, 'I haven't come to tell you off, John, but there are a few things I want to say because you and Brenda are so dear to us.

'Look at what the Lord has done these last few years! Great things have happened; the work has gone forward so much that it takes my breath away. Now, I see that a good deal of that has been down to you two – you have both had vision, you have worked hard together, your love for the Lord and for each other is amazing, it's what makes you a good team, and dear colleagues to work with.

'However, we are concerned about your workload, brother. Think of your radio series "Marriage, the Family and Morality" – what would you have said in one of your programmes about what happened on the day of the fiesta? You must have time for your family, John. Your children are growing up and they need you, too.'

We sat in silence through all that Bruce had to say. John was the first to speak in response. 'Thank you, Bruce. This interview must have cost you, and I am grateful to you. I value what you are saying and I take it to heart.'

How I wish with all my heart that John truly had taken

on board all the things Bruce had said; but instead he was rather cross with me for having talked to Joyce in the first place. There was a cloud between us now that was hard to cope with. Sadly – and wrongly – I, too, was very angry and my bitterness and resentment only grew. I was so self-righteous and it left me drained and estranged from my Lord.

I was entering an awful wilderness experience that was to last for a long time.

Rita's baby was due soon and she didn't want to go up to Quito to have her. 'What about a clinic here in Santo Dom?', I said. 'No,' she said, 'I want you to deliver me.' I told her I wasn't a qualified midwife and reminded her that this was her first baby. In the event, Amanda turned out to be presenting feet-first, so John had to go into town and fetch a doctor, who told us it was one of the worst presentations he had ever dealt with.

Nevertheless, Amanda emerged eventually, and after that everything was normal – although she didn't settle well for weeks, which nearly drove her parents mad!

Our time for furlough was approaching at the end of 1971. We were going home for Christmas, so we began to get ready, buying little mementos for the family. I was preparing myself for the change of scene and thinking about how it would affect the children.

They were so excited about it all. They were going to fly on a plane, they were going to meet their grandma and grandpa, aunties and uncles and cousins – and Mary Jane said she was going to see the Queen of England, which made us all laugh.

Susie, my original Spanish teacher, made me and the two little girls a sky-blue outfit each. Mine was a trouser suit, the girls each got a dress. For Matthew she made a lovely, brightly coloured shirt, and we bought him some new trousers.

Susie and her husband still came to church. She had become a really committed Christian, but Eduardo was still hesitating. Although he rarely missed a service, it was hard to know what was going on with him.

A 19-year-old Ecuadorian called Guido Tapia was travelling to England with us. He was a very clever and gifted fellow, who John had been teaching English for several years. His family were strong Catholics and it was difficult to know what he thought about church or faith – he would never discuss the subject with John. He wanted to study in England and we influenced him to go into nursing.

What courage and ambition Guido showed! He was to prove a model student and succeeded in everything he put his mind to. He completed his nursing course with a speciality in HIV/Aids. Many years later, when he went back to Ecuador to visit his family, he would help our son, Matthew, in Orphaids.

He married an English girl and they went to Mexico, where he did a degree in Latin American studies. He and Ann went on to have twin girls and a boy, and they now have three grandchildren as well. We are all still in contact.

Our journey home was quite exhausting: we had to wait hours in various different airports and with three little children that was very hard. It was exciting to see family and friends once again when we arrived, but those positive feelings were not to last. England had not had good associations for me ever since 1965, and I had not been looking forward to returning there.

We were renting a cottage for six months in a very small village in the depths of the countryside. Once more, I was abandoned, alone with our three children while John became distant and preoccupied with business. I felt neglected and angry.

Chapter 13

By the time we returned to Ecuador in June 1972 I was very unhappy, and in a bad spiritual state. I was further upset to find out that John had arranged to relieve a missionary couple in Cuenca, a city in the high Andes. There had been some discussion of this in England, but he certainly hadn't talked through the details with me.

His idea was that we would be looking after some underprivileged teens and twenty-year-olds, who were to study in a bilingual high school. I felt that our care of our own children – Mary Jane was now eight, Matthew five and AnaMari three – was being compromised. Also, although my walk with the Lord was far from what it should have been, I sensed we were not in his will there.

We were looking after maybe 18 young people every day. It was difficult to maintain harmony in the house, and the lack of privacy for us as a family was horrendous. John was still distant with me and we had little time to talk alone.

I find it difficult to put into words the horrid emotions I felt. I became more and more distressed and resentful. I was feeling very alone, and I felt a tremendous amount of guilt as well, on account of my anger and pride. I was unable to confide in John, which was partly my fault; and I neglected my times with the Lord. Sadly, I confess, I was furious with *him*, too, for the awfulness of the situation.

In short, I was in rebellion – but I was also cynical in my thinking, something I had never experienced before. It seemed to me that all of us who professed to be Christians were phonies, pretending to be Christians but knowingly breaking God's law. It was like a twisted self-righteousness: I was in mental and spiritual pain.

Besides this, without really being aware of it, I was very sick physically. I was reacting badly to the altitude –

so badly that in 1973 I suffered a cardiac arrest.

My heart had been racing for some months. We had gone to see a cardiologist who had been quite dismissive and said that as long as I didn't overdo things I would acclimatise eventually. Unfortunately, some time later I slipped and fell while carrying a tray of drinks and the shock of it stopped my heart. John resuscitated me, apparently with difficulty, but I found out afterwards that for several weeks I was only semi-conscious.

I was quite an invalid for a few months: I lost a lot of weight and became quite weak. David and Rita and their family were going back to England for Christmas and home assignment, so it was quickly arranged that I would travel back with them to get examined and treated.

I have said that we had many frightening experiences in the years we lived in Ecuador. To be honest, most of them run together in my memory, but one still stands out.

In early December, thanks to our friendship with the British ambassador, John and I received an invitation to attend a garden party in Quito in honour of Princess Anne and her new husband, Captain Mark Phillips. They were on honeymoon in the Galápagos Islands and would be spending some time in the capital before going back to England.

We accepted and made plans about what we would wear. John would need a formal suit and I a nice dress. I was easily sorted, as I was able to have something to my liking made in Santo Dom, but we could not get a suit for John there.

We were told that the best suits in Ecuador were made in Guayaquil. John wanted me to go with him in the Land Rover – he thought I would know better than him what to choose. We arranged for Elvia to join Gladis for the day, as the children knew the two girls well and they were all very fond of each other.

We set off very early, and the trip in the car together

was such a treat that I remember the time seemed to pass very quickly. John knew of a safe place to park and we had an early lunch so that once we had the suit we could get back on the road without delay.

We became a little dispirited after we had visited two shops and still not found what we were looking for. John said: 'Let's try one more and if we can't find anything, we'll leave it and go home.'

We had no more success in the third shop, so we gave up. We were just starting out on our way back to the car when we found ourselves surrounded by three youths with knives. They were very threatening – one of them was yelling at John that they would stab me in front of him if we didn't do as they said.

One of them emptied my handbag onto the pavement while another went through John's pockets. They took his wallet and all his money, our watches and a gold cross and chain I was wearing. All the while, we were trembling with fear because we had heard of people being killed by muggers.

When they were done, they ran off as fast as could be. I was suddenly filled with rage and shouted in English: 'You pigs! You cowardly pigs!' There is a very powerful fly-killer in Ecuador called Piks and everyone around us thought that is what I was shouting and they found it very funny.

The owner of the shop came out and invited us to come back in and sit down and have some coffee. Everyone was very kind to us. The owner told us: 'You were very lucky – we have seen people stabbed to death on this street.'

Once we had recovered, we set off again. John didn't think we had enough petrol to get us home, but he knew where the office of the Bible Society was and we went there and borrowed some money. When we returned to the car, John said: 'Let's thank the Lord for his protection today, and pray for those poor youths who attacked us!' I realised that his feelings were right and mine were so wrong! When we prayed for those boys, my heart was touched and I asked the Lord to forgive me.

Back in Santo Dom, we told Bruce and Joyce what had happened and their reaction was the same as John's. A few days later, they gave us a gift of money towards the cost of the new suit, which in the end we bought in Quito.

At the garden party, Peter Mennell rather took us under his wing – I think he thought us extremely brave people! – and he made a point of bringing Princess Anne and Captain Phillips over to meet us. John, as a joke, invited her down to Santo Dom to see what we were up to and, to my surprise, she replied: 'Not bloody likely! You won't get me going down those mountain roads.'

Leaving my children and my husband to go to England was the most agonising thing I have ever had to do. I was distraught as I got on the plane to fly to Quito.

Much to my amazement, John joined me there the next morning. He had travelled overnight to see me off (it seems he didn't have enough money to come on the flight with me, so he took a 10-hour bus ride). I was so thrilled to see him, and was comforted.

He wanted to tell me how much he loved me and how he felt he had failed me dreadfully, neglecting to look after me as he should. He was very sorry. We hugged each other and prayed together that the Lord would take care of us and our children. We promised to write often and be in touch as much as possible.

John and his brother David had arranged for me to stay with a nurse friend in Bury St Eds. I saw a doctor there as soon as possible and very early in 1974 I was put into Papworth, a specialist cardiac hospital in Cambridge. I was to remain there for two months or so, I think, and then I was to have six weeks' rehabilitation.

David was so kind to me, for which I was very thankful. He took care of the finances of my stay in England, and he came to see me a few times, too.

I had been staying in the hospital for quite a while when I had some visitors from a local church who left me some books. I read them and the Spirit of God started to move in my heart. I then got back into the scriptures and began again to hear the Lord's voice, loud and clear.

My hard, bitter heart began to melt. The Holy Spirit was convicting me constantly. Psalm 19:7–14 in particular had a profound effect on me, and especially the last three verses:

> Forgive my hidden faults.
> Keep your servant also from wilful sins;
>   may they not rule over me.
> Then I will be blameless,
>   innocent of great transgression.
> May these words of my mouth and this
>   meditation of my heart
>   be pleasing in your sight,
> LORD, my Rock and my Redeemer.

This psalm is so powerful and it made me realise just how far I had fallen. I came to see my attitude and behaviour as wilful sin against my wonderful God.

I became more broken and knew such anguish of soul! I cried out to the Lord, my Saviour, who I had wounded so dreadfully, who was so grieved by the state I was in – and he heard my cries. What a relief it was to confess everything, to tell him how sorry I was for my bad spirit and the awful resentment I had been feeling towards my husband!

There were other issues, too. How guilty I had been of deceit! I had been breaking God's law of love and forgiveness. I had become quite flippant, too. Who was I to criticise other Christians? I had become very critical of other people, both in Ecuador and in England – but most of all of John.

How forgiving is our God! I sensed his glorious presence, his cleansing, his overwhelming forgiveness and a peace that only he can give. He restored to me the joy of my salvation. My trust in him grew and it was like having a new encounter with God and knowing him in a more intimate way.

I had such a wonderful, humbling sense of his nearness and love, filling my being and my days. I made a sacred promise that I would never wilfully deceive anyone again.

There were many letters I had to write, to ask various people to forgive me for being so judgemental and bitter.

I received in return such lovely letters! Some said that they hadn't realised I had had such feelings. The letters from John were just amazing: he thought that he had been far from loving and understanding, and that this was the real cause of much of our estrangement, and he wondered how I could still love him.

What grateful joy was mine, to know everyone's forgiveness and to have so many relationships restored! The Lord showed himself to me in so many different ways, and my heart was filled with his peace. He 'crowned me with love and compassion' (Psalm 103:4) and filled my days with praise.

One verse that made a particular impact on me was Proverbs 16:6:

> Through love and faithfulness sin is
>   atoned for;
>   through the fear of the LORD evil is
>   avoided.

I promised the Lord I would obey his words of wisdom – and with his grace I have been faithful in keeping that promise to this very day.

It was two weeks or so later that the doctor who had charge of me told me he and his colleagues thought that John ought to be there. They felt that he needed to understand what had happened to me and to grasp that we both had to realise our limitations and manage our working lives accordingly.

He was asked to come as soon as possible, and was able to leave the children in the care of a young nurse from America, Dona Sensenig, who was working in the area as a midwife. (She did a fantastic job with them and they love her to this day – she is one of our whole family's best friends.)

How I missed my little ones! The pain of them being so far away was very distressing, and just wondering how they were would set me off crying.

When John arrived, the doctors sent us off for a week's holiday with friends in Kent (who I shall introduce properly in chapter 17). It allowed us to catch up with each other and enjoy being together again – and to talk frankly about the way we had both disobeyed the Lord.

When we returned to Cambridge, the doctors had some long conversations with us. Two of them felt that I shouldn't go back to Ecuador. The one who had had charge of me, who we saw on his own quite often, probed us about some of the factors he thought were contributing to the problem, and we both opened up to him and admitted that we knew that our lives had been far from what they should have been: obedient to the Lord, his word and the Holy Spirit.

John and I became incredibly close to each other once again. We loved one another, and we loved the Lord, so we waited for him to show us his will. Naturally, we both wanted to go back to Ecuador, but most important of all for us was submission to the Lord's will for us. So, we waited to hear what the doctors had decided and felt we must be guided by that.

It was eventually agreed by all of them that I could and should return to Ecuador – but not to high altitude or to work that would overly stress us as a family. The doctor who had had charge of me, who was by now a good friend, impressed on John that he must look after me more; and, when he received that assurance, said that he was sure we would be fine and wished us every happiness.

We duly went back, with great gladness, in late May or June (I think) after my rehabilitation. We collected our three darling children and returned to Santo Dom, where we were to enjoy four wonderful years in service together. God's work went on from strength to strength – and our family life was a delight!

Chapter 14

We felt much more at home in Santo Dom. Abdon and
Doreen were there, and so were Bruce and Joyce. The
house Fausto had built for us four years ago was too far
from town, but the Moores were shortly going on home
assignment and so the plan was that we would live in the
clinic until they left and then move into their house until
they came back. This made us so happy!

El Buen Pastor was still going strong but there were
under-currents of unease about certain things that were
happening. This was mainly to do with discipline: some
members had been put out of fellowship because of trivial
mistakes, which could have been sorted out with good
pastoral care and help.

However, the Ecuadorians in our eldership were very
strict, bordering on the unloving and legalistic. This was
to prove so problematic at times – the leadership really
needed a better understanding of what the Bible teaches
about such matters.

Because I had been separated from our little ones so
long, the team felt that for a few weeks I should be given
time to care for them first and foremost. My absence, and
then John's, had unsettled them and they needed us both
– but principally me.

So, I started home-schooling them in earnest, and we
also had a lot of close family times, doing fun things. In
the evenings, after they had got ready for bed, we cuddled
up together in the double bed and I read to them. The
first book I read was *Little Pilgrim's Progress*. They so
loved that story, I would catch them 'being Pilgrim' when
they were playing together outside.

AnaMari came to faith through that book a year or so
later, after she read it again herself.

Mary Jane was nearly 10 now and she needed to apply
herself more to her schooling, so I had to be disciplined

and not allow myself to take on things that could get in the way. As I am far from well educated myself, I often felt out of my depth – though at least as a bookworm I was widely read.

I did some play-type schooling with Matthew, too. We didn't send our children to the local school chiefly because we were anxious that they should be able to speak English as well as they spoke Spanish.

As well as our children, we had brought back from Cuenca a girl called Angelita. She had been horribly neglected and abused and so some nuns had asked John whether we could take care of her. We weren't sure how old she was, but a doctor friend said he thought she was 11 or 12. She was not even registered as a citizen and didn't have a surname, so we had to get papers for her, which involved queueing for hours in government offices.

It was obvious she had been severely undernourished – she had bow legs and other skeletal signs of rickets – but what she needed most of all was lots of love. Our children were very affectionate and caring to her, and so were John and I.

Angelita adored our children. Because she couldn't read, Mary Jane tried to teach her, and I began to educate her slowly, too. She found it difficult to retain anything, but with time and perseverance she did eventually learn to read. To give her a little money of her own, we paid her to help with the household chores, which she loved to do.

There were new things happening in the church that made me glad. Joyce and Doreen had started a choir, which I joined and I loved my involvement in it. Also, the music group they had had before we went on furlough was much bigger and better now.

The church had a number of new members who were rather better educated and they were able to help quite a lot in many ways. Some of them were our own age and had children the same age as ours, so there was much more of a social dimension to our lives than there was in our first term as missionaries. John now realised that he needed to take care that he didn't become a workaholic again and of course that greatly enhanced our family life.

Fausto was by now married, to a girl called Maria who was also from the high Andes. They were such a lovely couple – and to this day they are two of our very best Ecuadorian friends.

I was meant to deliver their first baby, but over the weekend Maria went into labour I had the flu. I was running a high fever and was unable to stand, so John delivered her instead – a daughter they named Suni. After the emergency of AnaMari's birth, I had insisted on him assisting me several times just to build up his confidence, and fortunately Suni's delivery was quite straightforward.

John was eager to start a Gideons network, as some of our members were now professionals or businesspeople. The town had grown considerably since we first arrived and by now there were many schools, colleges, hotels and other establishments in Santo Dom that they could get the word of God into.

Once these local Christians understood the vision, they became really keen and did fantastic work. Their wives were very involved, too – and in fact we all became great friends.

John and I were still needed to teach people how to care for themselves and their children and so once more we were doing medical work. The family-planning programme, which had been on hold in our absence, was soon up and running again. John set himself the task of persuading the local health bodies to get involved in this and promote it; it took a lot of patience and time, but in the end they took it on. By the time we left Ecuador in 1978, it had become a national organisation.

I still delivered babies, but as there were now some

good clinics in the town I did so only for the very poor people. It amuses me that today there are so many little Brenditas in Santo Dom.

We had not been back for more than a couple of months when the time came for the Moores to return to the States for a while. They were going to be involved in some way in translating the scriptures into Tsafiki, but they were not sure how long they would be away.

Someone who had helped them ever since he was a boy was a young Colorado man called Primitivo. He was a firm Christian and a remarkable fellow, highly respected by the tribe but still humble despite being the most educated of them. Today, he is a pastor of one of their churches.

The church did a 'sending home' service for Bruce and Joyce. There was lots of singing, including both soloists and the choir. The Colorados were there in large numbers, so we sang some of their songs in their language, too, and everyone seemed to have an encouraging message for everyone else. All in all, it was an amazing occasion!

After Bruce and Joyce had left, we were able to move into their house. It was quite spacious, with three large bedrooms, an office, a big kitchen-cum-dining-room and a sitting room. It was made of wood and part of it stood on stilts.

John put up bunk beds in the office for Matthew and AnaMari; Angelita and Mary Jane shared the second of the bedrooms, and the third was occupied by a new member of the household, Rosie.

She was a young Christian girl, from a farm out in the sticks, who needed to live in town in order to finish her studies. She gave me some help around the house, out of the goodness of her heart. She was getting married the following year, so she was not with us that long. We all loved Rosie and how we missed her when she left us!

John was back on the radio again – his earlier talks on marriage, the family and morality had proved to be very popular and so the local station was broadcasting them again, with John now answering listeners' questions in a live phone-in after each programme.

He also did most of the teaching in El Buen Pastor. Abdon preached quite often, and others were being trained – though not to the depth John would have liked.

Baptisms were great occasions enjoyed by everyone in the church. We would all pile into a big truck belonging to one of the fellowship and drive to a large river, a tradition we had started back in 1969. Usually there were many people getting baptised, and afterwards there would be food and drink for all.

Our own children were baptised in Ecuador in due course.

Christmas came and was a happy time both in the church and in our family. We had been able to get a few extra special things for the children while we were in England. Also, a dear lady in Cambridge called Anne Knappett had given me a Tiny Tears doll that her daughter had grown out of – and bought a second one to go with it. They had clothes as well! Mary Jane and AnaMari – now 10 and six respectively – were thrilled with them. John wrote their names on the dolls' bottoms, much to their amusement. Matthew, too, had some lovely presents, sent by family in England.

Our children now had to be allowed time to play with their new friends at church, which was difficult to arrange because the other children went to school. We managed, but sometimes they or their friends were disappointed and there were tears.

It was not far into 1975 when we heard that two young women from Cambridge would like to come for a year or so to help us in whatever way they could. Christina (who was known as Tinie, pronounced 'teeny') was 18 and on her gap year before studying occupational therapy; Vivian (or Vivvie) was a few years older and was taking a break from her job as a schoolteacher to see some overseas Christian mission. I think they knew each other from church.

I have mentioned that part of the Moores' house stood on stilts – Bruce used the space underneath as a garage for his Jeep. We turned this area into a room for the two of them with a wooden floor, some makeshift walls and mesh windows; and bought beds and other bits and bobs to make them comfortable.

We gave them a week to make themselves at home before we put them to work. Between them, they would be taking over doing school with Mary Jane, Matthew and AnaMari, and would also help generally in the church.

Tinie was quiet and thoughtful, though very warm and friendly; Vivvie was more confident and outgoing. They both settled in well and soon had school going. Their programme was varied and fun and the two older children really enjoyed their lessons. They introduced 'physical jerks' as well, which Mary Jane didn't like but Matthew loved.

What happiness those two women brought us! They experienced so much during their time with us, and our children thought they were wonderful.

Life was quite busy. John and an Ecuadorian called Enrique ran El Buen Pastor along with Abdon, Fausto and some other men. Doreen was involved, too, though like her husband she naturally gave more time to the Colorados.

The construction of the new church was now nearly finished, and what a lovely building it was – it was enormous! However, there were some gaps between the top of the circular wall and the roof and we had a bit of trouble with things like birds and mosquitos flying in.

Sometimes we would get a swarm of locusts, which I hated! On one occasion, I managed to create an uproar. We were all standing to sing one Sunday morning when a locust flew up my skirt! I had a real phobia about the things and so I freaked and started flapping my skirt can-can style. In the end, I was so embarrassed I ran outside.

One of the elders came out to see how I was and found me a bit tearful. 'Oh, Brenda,' he said, 'don't cry! The people were not laughing at you really, but the way you flapped your skirt was just so comical!'

Rosie left us around March to get married. As she went to live with her new husband in the sierra, high in the mountains, we didn't see her very often after that, but we never forgot her!

A little later, we were joined by a very charming young man, a Canadian contact of John's who had come to have a look at mission abroad. He was quite tall, slim and blond and we all found him easy to be with.

His name was Matthew and so the local people called him 'Mateito' ('dear little Mateo'), just as they did our son – which was rather funny as he was so tall compared with everyone else. In our home, he was known as 'Mateo *grande*' ('big Matthew') and our Matthew as 'Mateo *chiquito*' (meaning 'small').

John received an invitation to tour the Brethren assemblies in Canada, both to do some teaching and to promote the work we were doing. He said he might be gone for up to three months.

I told him that if he was convinced it was the Lord's will, he could go with my blessing. The fact that we had Tinie, Vivvie and Mateo Grande with us meant that his family would not be alone or at risk.

So, John went off. He was travelling around Canada on the long-distance bus network, which was the cheapest way to do it, and so he saw a lot of the country. We heard from him quite frequently and he said he was missing us all very much.

About a month after he went, we had a problem with the toilet, which was in the Moores' yard. This was simply a hole in the ground with a box over it topped off with a toilet seat and a lid. Suddenly, we found that we had swarms of flies for company when we were down there – it really was awful! I put some lime down and that helped for a while – but not much.

Mateo Grande decided that he would deal with the problem. Without saying anything to me, he poured a load of petrol down the hole and threw in a piece of burning wood. Those of us in the house leapt to our feet when we heard a loud bang and saw the roof of the loo flying into the air. Mateo Grande was standing there, covered with soot and who knows what else! After the initial shock, we just could not stop laughing.

Unfortunately, that did not solve the problem, so we got some men in to dig a new hole and build a new toilet over it. In the meantime, we had to brave the old one as best we could.

Bruce and Joyce were coming back for six weeks or so, so we rented some accommodation on the edge of town – I'll explain why in the next chapter. It was a very nice bungalow made of breeze block, and there was plenty of room for us all.

The only downside was that the ceilings were quite low. The rains had just started and this meant that we had to put up clothes lines indoors to dry our washing; and as there were seven or eight females in all in our household, there were always a lot of panties hanging up. Mateo Grande had us all in stitches as he brushed his head against them every time he walked through the room.

What fun that young man was!

Chapter 15

Around the time that John was to leave for Canada,
he was approached with regard to the piece of land we
owned and the two houses we had built on it. He had
already sold half an acre the previous year, to pay for his
flight to join me in England, and we had been renting out
the rest while we lived in the Moores' house, which had
provided us with a very small income.

Now a man wanted to buy it. We didn't know him, but
he was a Christian who was well known to others in the
fellowship. After praying about it, we agreed to sell up. I
loved our house and the land around it, but I couldn't
face being there alone with the children, and away from
all the activity around the church, while John was abroad.

Not long after, a piece of land opposite the church
came on the market. With the funds we now had we were
able to buy it and start building a breeze-block house.
John's Aunty Lily helped us with a small gift of money
and we took things slowly.

The bungalow we were renting meanwhile was called
'Primavera' ('Spring') and, as I have said, was really nice.
However, I have one awful memory associated with it.

There had been some troubling political wrangles
going on, and also a student uprising, and the police and
the army were everywhere. When a march by the students
in Santo Dom arrived in the main plaza, they were shot
at indiscriminately and many of them were killed on the
spot, and others died later. The whole town was plunged
into mourning! It took years to get over it.

Here is a much happier memory from that period.
One day, I thought I could hear a cat mewing outside the
house. I was curious, because people don't keep cats in
Ecuador as they don't do well in that climate. I went to
investigate – and a few feet from our front door I found

a baby in a cardboard box! I couldn't believe my eyes. I picked it up and took it inside, and the others were as shocked as I was. Mary Jane jumped up and down and clapped her hands. 'Oh, Mammy,' she cried, 'we've got to look after it, Jesus has given it to us.'

'It' was a *mestizo* boy, about two months old. The older girls looked after the little chap while I went out to report my find to the authorities and buy some suitable food and some clothes and nappies. When I got back, I made up some feeds and then, with Mary Jane's help, Tinie and Vivvie fed him, bathed him and dressed him while AnaMari and Mateo Chiquito looked on wide-eyed.

The baby was healthy and looked well cared for, and soon went to sleep. So far he had been no problem at all.

I soon got into the routine of looking after him. The older girls wanted to be Mum, too, so they took it in turns to feed him in the day and I dealt with him in the night. The authorities sent someone to visit us and they begged us to care for him until they could sort something out.

Some missionaries up in Quito heard about him – possibly Doreen had said something. There was an American missionary couple who wanted to adopt a baby, so it was arranged that they would come and see him. They fell in love with him instantly – but they had to leave him with us for a while longer until they had all the papers and other legalities sorted.

John arrived home from Canada a week or so after the baby came to us, and was a bit put out at first; but the baby himself won him over!

Not long after John's return, we were able to move back into Bruce and Joyce's house. We were all happy to be near the church again.

While John had been travelling around Canada by bus, he had set himself the task of learning the whole of Hebrews in Spanish by heart, and when he got back to Santo Dom he began a series of sermons (or perhaps 'lessons' would be a better word) on Sunday mornings. They were the most powerful I had ever heard him preach. I was challenged by them, and so many others have commented on those messages years later, saying how blessed they were by them.

Time flies when life is good and now the moment had come when Tinie and Vivvie had to return home. They had really loved their stay with us and we had become so fond of them, it would be very different without them.

We had a special meal to say our goodbyes and spent the evening sharing our thoughts and memories with each other. John made some funny remark about them having to put up with me for so long, and Tinie said: 'Oh, John! How Brenda copes with everyone and everything is amazing. So many people take her for granted!'

That night, when we were in bed, John asked me: 'Do *I* take you for granted?' 'I've never thought so,' I replied, 'but I suppose there's a tendency for husbands and wives to do so. I know I sometimes take *you* for granted.

'Don't take it to heart, John!', I said. 'Tinie is still only 19, she doesn't know the dynamics of married life. She's become very fond of me and the children, and also she's seen more of what I do than what you do. She sees how much everyone appreciates and admires you compared with me, and she feels deeply about it. I've told her that that is part of being a missionary wife – not to mention Ecuador's patriarchal culture.'

Life goes on and there is always change. After Tinie and Vivvie went, we suffered withdrawal symptoms for a couple of months. We all missed them so much!

We also had to give the baby to his adoptive parents, although we had become so very fond of him – especially me! They came to collect him and told us they had named him Matthew after our son, which he was thrilled about.

Mary Jane wanted to go to school like the local kids, so we decided that once AnaMari was old enough we would let them all go together. It was a private school, highly rated by people who had children there, and it was a new adventure when in due course AnaMari joined reception and the other two entered their appropriate years.

We were still staying in Bruce and Joyce's house, even though they were back in the country. They were living in Quito now and when Bruce needed to be in Santo Dom he would travel down and stay with us.

Our new house was going up fast – the inside was now complete and pretty much all that was left to do was some finishing off on the outside. However, there was still some scaffolding up, and loads of rubble lying around. John had given the children instructions that they were not to go near the new house without an adult.

Unfortunately, Mary Jane decided they should play a game nearby and once they were there she wanted to see what was up the scaffolding. She got to the top and then turned to come down, but missed her footing and fell and injured her arm. 'Don't tell Mammy or Daddy!', she begged the others, but she was in a lot of pain and so Matthew came running to find us in the church and told us, in tears: 'We've been naughty and Mary Jane is hurt.'

One look at her arm and we knew it was broken, just above the wrist. 'This means a trip to Quito,' John said, so we gave her painkillers and put her arm on a pillow and we all set off on the three-hour bus journey to the capital. John felt that we all needed to go with Mary Jane to give her the moral support she would need. He told me her bones would need setting and that could be quite painful – and he was right!

Eventually we were all back home, with Mary Jane tucked up in bed with her arm in plaster. John gave her another day to recuperate and then the following day, after breakfast and morning devotions, he said to the children: 'We have to talk about what happened when Mary Jane was hurt. Have you got anything to say first before I begin?'

All three together said they were sorry they had been disobedient, and Mary Jane added: 'Daddy, it was all my fault. It was my idea to go there and go up the scaffolding, and I'm truly sorry.'

John caught my eye, as much as to say: What can I say to that? 'Well, lovely daughter,' he replied, 'I'm so glad that you admit your wrongdoing and that you are all so sorry about it. Mammy and I forgive you, but let this be a lesson to you: there are consequences when we are disobedient. However,' he added, 'on this occasion I think you have had enough punishment.'

What a real moral lesson that was! How easily as Christians we are disobedient and stray: we go further than we intended, and many people are affected and even the innocent may be deeply hurt.

The house was completed towards the end of 1977 and we moved in just after Christmas.

John felt that, as our fellowship was growing, it was losing that sense of being a family. He believed that the leadership should have the evangelistic vision to see where we could and should plant new churches, but sadly the other elders didn't want any of our members to go and worship somewhere else.

John was a very patient and determined man (albeit a quiet one), so every so often he would bring up this proposal again. We prayed about it for what seemed to be ages, and eventually Fausto offered to lead in planting a new church. Slowly, the other elders came round to the idea and so began the planting of daughter churches around the town. A number were up and running before our current term in Ecuador came to an end and it was time for us to return to England for a while.

Our four years back in Santo Dom had been such an amazingly happy time for us both, especially in our family life. John and I were so united in the work, so close in heart and mind, and our children had been a real joy, too. How blessed we had been!

As the time drew near for us to go home, we knew we had a huge decision to make about our children's education. We believed that they needed to know their own country and culture, and most of all their own language, better. Eventually, we came to the conclusion that it would be right to remain in England for as long as was needed to give our children a decent start in life.

Mary Jane was now 13 and AnaMari was nine, and Matthew would be 11 next April, so that would mean that the two older ones would be in secondary school and AnaMari would still be in primary. We planned to be back in England at the beginning of July, in good time for the start of the new school year in September.

It was with a heavy heart that I began our packing, and often I was in tears. Our family life had always been a nightmare in England and whenever we went back for any reason I was very afraid – essentially because of the awful loneliness I always suffered. For me, it was as if we became a one-parent family whenever we lived there.

Nonetheless, God told me to trust him, that he would use us as a family to his glory. He gave me a picture in my mind's eye (which is something I had never experienced before). I saw a house like a doll's house; the sky behind it was dark, but light was streaming from every window and from the open front door, where John and I were standing with his arm around me.

I was amazed and comforted. It was a very vivid picture and I knew it to be from the Lord. The message was: Your family will be blessed, and your life together will be like a light set on a hill.

I told John of my sense of dread and the extraordinary reassurance God had given me. His response was: 'Oh, you're just like me, you're just sad to be leaving Ecuador!

'What have we to fear in England?'

Chapter 16

Sadly, my fears were not unfounded. By October, it had all begun again: John was out a lot and became more and more detached from us. At almost 14, Mary Jane was especially alert, but all three of the children noticed the way his whole personality was changing and they were asking me for answers to some very difficult questions.

They were miserable and longed to be back in Ecuador where Dad – and life – was normal. They were having a very hard time adapting to English culture; their school life was challenging, and even the food, when we were invited out, tasted so bland to them!

Christmas, especially, was not a happy time. I kept myself together by remembering that wonderful picture God had given me in Ecuador, of a house flooded with light, and I'd ask: 'What is going on, Lord? This situation is nothing like that!'

Once again, in desperation I cried out: 'Lord, it's so difficult when I know something awful is happening!' Once again, he replied: 'Brenda, trust me! I hear your prayers, and I am in control.'

In the months that followed, John seemed to be more and more frustrated with us all. He became increasingly unhappy and bad-tempered. The strained atmosphere was exhausting for all of us, and really painful at times. Our children wanted to go back to Ecuador and said so often.

In May 1979, John had to return there. There were problems over our house there and it could be very time-consuming to sort out the legalities in a country that at the time was going through enormous economic upheaval, to the extent that some banks were having to foreclose. It was imperative that he was there. (In fact, we were to lose all the money we had in sucres.)

Unfortunately, after only five weeks, he was called back to England because his mother, his eldest brother and I were involved in a nasty car accident. Mum Hart had very bad head injuries and was unconscious, while Joseph had some damage to his sternum and I had a fractured scapula, bruised ribs and a dislocated shoulder. I had also been briefly unconscious, and I developed a chest infection. (I was still feeling wretched a couple of months later.)

I was out of hospital and home again when John got back, so I tried hard to get back to normal. I started physio and the movement in my shoulder was improving and I was slowly getting better.

Sadly, once again John began to be out a lot. I understood that he needed to visit his mother often, but he would be gone for hours and he never phoned to let me know why, or where he had gone or what he was doing or when he would be home. It was so unlike my dear John that it became unbearable.

Things got so bad that in the end I felt I had no choice but to bring things to a head. I told the Lord that I was feeling very frightened and vulnerable and I asked him for guidance.

Our children were on holiday from school at the time and were going to spend two weeks away at Christian camps. They left on a Saturday and the following evening John preached at a local church. It was then that God began to guide me.

While my husband was speaking, I realised that he was no longer walking with the Lord, that his heart was in rebellion. He was certainly not practising what he preached that night. I came away really hurting, crying out to God inside to have mercy on my family. As we drove back in silence, I prayed: 'Please give me wisdom and courage! Something has to happen tonight.'

As soon as we had arrived home and taken our coats off, I challenged John about the message he had given that evening. I asked him: 'Would you like to know how your sermon struck me? I thought it was all hypocrisy. If you truly believe what you said tonight, how come you are behaving like someone who is not even a Christian, let alone a leader and teacher?'

I told him that our children were asking why he was being so cruel, to me and to them. 'I can't live with any more pain,' I said. 'You seem oblivious to the enormity of your behaviour. I don't want my children to have a father who causes them pain with his inability to grow up, face reality and be the man of God he professes to be but is not.

'Our marriage is in jeopardy,' I went on. 'The way you have been behaving this last year has caused me such anguish! Things are so serious, we are going to have to go and see someone in real authority in the church.'

In a broken voice, John agreed. He admitted that he was in a real spiritual crisis. We wept a lot that night. Our emotions were so raw that neither of us could comfort the other.

The very next morning, I told John that he had to take me to see our dear friend Victor Jack. As we were going to get in the car, I asked him: 'Do you really want our marriage?'

At that question, John's face became so distressed it looked as if he'd been winded. He raised his hands in the air and said, with a catch in his voice: 'Brenda, more than anything else in the world I want our marriage and our lovely children. I haven't shown much love to you and the children lately, but you are truly loved by me. To lose you would be the end of me as a person.

'When I married you, it was for as long as we live. I do love you, very much, and always have.' Then he asked: 'Do *you* still want our marriage?'

At that moment, I couldn't answer. In my heart I wanted to fulfil my vows to him and to the Lord, but I was thinking: 'How can I cope? How can I and the children go on suffering like we have this last year? Will John come out of this crisis?' I was in such mental pain, it was almost unbearable.

John started to drive and as soon as we were on a fairly straight road I began to bare my soul to him.

'We've been in this situation before,' I said, 'in 1965. I was willing to forgive your neglect and the huge pain it caused me then, but when it recurred in late 1971 and '72 it was the beginning of almost a complete breakdown for me. I felt so diminished, so embittered and angry with God, and completely messed up spiritually.

'I was to blame for my sins and woes, but you were supposed to be the head of our family and you were in a very bad place, too. When the head of the family has serious spiritual issues, what hope is there for the family? Of course the Lord is our hope – but that means there has to be obedience and trust.

'Here we are again, in England, suffering this awful estrangement. I'm feeling so confused, so heartbroken that I'm not *sure* you mean what you say.

'Our children are now growing up,' I continued. 'Mary Jane will be 15 this Christmas and she is making a lot of difficult adjustments to a very different culture, which unlike the Latin culture is hard and undemonstrative. A girl that age notices things, so think how she has been affected by your utterly selfish behaviour! She is really hurt by your evident regard for others and your lack of regard for us.

'I know that Mattie and AnaMari have been hurt, too. You were their hero and you have let them down. They see that you no longer show me the concern and respect you used to. They see how you have hurt me and let me down so often, especially since my accident.

'All I have heard from our kids for months is how unhappy they are, especially with your strange, restless behaviour. You have neglected them and me abysmally!'

I had always given John a lot of freedom over the years to live his own life, much more than many other wives would have done; but when I did confront him, I spoke my mind like a proper Northerner.

John was very subdued and I could see he was hurting, so I was quiet for some time.

Later, I said sadly: 'In Ecuador, we were such a happy family! England is a place I have come to associate only with pain.' There was a very long silence after that.

Then John responded, brokenly: 'I understand how you feel, Brenda. Everything you have said is right, and I am so very, very sorry. Is it possible that you could forgive me all over again? I realise that my behaviour, humanly speaking, has been unforgivable. I feel so wretched about it all!'

At this, I began to cry. I didn't say anything, but inside I was thinking: I want to forgive him and I know that I should, but... How do I know that in a few years' time he won't relapse?

'John,' I said, 'am *I* your problem? Do I fail you in some way? Do you really love me, or are you just being a dutiful Christian husband with a sham marriage? I couldn't bear to be married to someone who was not truly happy with me and didn't really want to be with me and was just living with me to keep up appearances.

'That would be living a lie – and I will not live a lie!'

John said emphatically: 'You are certainly not the problem!' With tears in his voice, he continued: 'You have been the best wife any man could have. You must never feel that any of this is your fault. I am my own worst enemy. I am a very frail, failing Christian, and before you and my God I am deeply sorry.'

We didn't talk much after that. I felt I had made it plain, as kindly as possible, that there were to be no half measures.

To begin with, I talked with Victor on my own. Telling him what I had been dealing with reduced me to tears, which he fully understood. John saw him a couple of hours later, and then we both saw him together.

He had a lot of things to say to us both. To me, he spoke about the need to forgive – I don't think he was then aware of the previous breakdowns in our relationship – while John sat there looking very contrite, his whole body expressing his shame and embarrassment. He admitted that the whole situation was entirely his fault.

Later that same evening, Victor impressed on John that feeling remorse was only the start – the proof of real repentance and deep sorrow for his sinful, self-centred behaviour would be a change in how he lived.

Some days later, John told me how very glad he was that his confused and rebellious state of mind and heart had ended and now he felt profoundly and wonderfully relieved. He said it was like being released from prison.

He pulled me into his arms, and held me so tight: 'Oh, Brenda! I can see now what we have been saved from, and in God's grace and forgiveness he has once more given me the chance to prove my love and commitment, first to him and then to you, my lovely wife, and our precious children.'

We both wept and hugged each other. His repentance was very real. In truth, his problem had been a spiritual one. It was something that had dogged him and that had to be dealt with once and for all.

We were full of gratitude that it was dealt with by the Lord so completely. It was a real humbling – it was like major surgery, like having a malignant growth removed. Involving Victor was just what we needed: it had been a real blessing to both of us.

I was only too happy to forgive John, he was so very broken. So was I – but in God's wonderful grace and love we were able to help each other to heal.

All this is more than 40 years ago now, and in all that time John never suffered such destructive attacks again. As a family, we came to love England.

John's brother David had known nothing of the trauma we had gone through. He and his wife, Brenda, and their two children were always there for us, but some things are very private. They must have been a bit bemused at how things were, especially when we decided to move to Kent when a God-directed opportunity came our way.

Some years later, after David suffered a major heart attack, the two brothers became very close.

We had some further times with Victor, which were a real joy. Within a few weeks, he took us through our marriage vows again, which we meant with all our hearts. The vow 'to love and to cherish' had a new significance for us.

The healing of emotional wounds takes time, but God's grace is sufficient. Once when I was talking to Victor on the phone, he reminded me of those lovely words in Isaiah 40:28ff:

> His understanding no one can fathom.
> He gives strength to the weary
>   and increases the power of the weak.
> ... Those who hope in the LORD
>   will renew their strength.
> They will soar on wings like eagles;
>   they will run and not grow weary,
>   they will walk and not be faint.

I would repeat those verses many times a day, and how true they were for me then and so often since!

For a long time, it seemed to me, I had been deeply distressed by John's spiritual breakdown. I had been in constant fear for almost a year and had shed many tears alone as I pleaded with the Lord to give me wisdom, which I felt I was sorely in need of.

I knew that I needed to trust my loving heavenly Father and I did, with all my heart – and he honoured that trust. But fear is exhausting, and the inevitable showdown had been emotionally and physically draining for me – and for John, too.

He found me one morning, after the children had gone to school, in a state of real anguish. He tried to comfort me but I could not be comforted – I needed to sob out my pain before my Lord and look to him for renewed strength and consolation.

John had to leave for work, but before he did he wrote this letter and left it propped up by the kettle:

> My dearest one
> I cannot go this morning without reassuring you again of my love for you.
>
> My darling, I do understand your present turmoil and never think that you are reproaching me. I know that you hate to tell me, but I prefer that you do – PLEASE.
>
> With God's help we can overcome together. Read Psalm 84: 'Blessed is the man whose strength is in thee ... passing through the valley of weeping they make it a place of springs, yea, the early rain covereth it with blessing, they go from strength to strength!!'
>
> I love you my sweetheart xx

Chapter 17

Life took off after that with a capital 'L'. From then on, John and I were at one again. Within just a few days, it seemed, we experienced such deep tenderness for each other, we had a renewed sense of how precious we were one to the other. Thus began God's wonderful healing of our relationship and his rich blessing of it.

It seemed that our love for each other had been honed, refined. We rediscovered the romance and the closeness we had known before we came back to England.

Both of us had been so deeply hurt by all that had happened, we needed to practise lots of *agapē* love as we recovered from the emotional trauma; but, in the words of the 18th-century hymn written by one of John's ancestors, Joseph Hart,

> How good is the God we adore,
> Our faithful, unchangeable Friend,
> Whose love is as great as His power,
> And knows neither measure nor end!

How we looked forward to a future serving that Lord together once more!

The first thing John did after the children got back from their camps was to resume our family devotions, which he had sadly let slip. (I had been doing something with the children in the evenings, but it was not the same as when Daddy did them – and they said so!)

They certainly noticed the difference. One evening, Mary Jane said: 'Daddy, you're your normal self again. You've been so nasty, you didn't seem like our daddy. What happened while we were away?'

Humbly and honestly, John gave them a very short and simple account. He admitted that he had lost his way and had been disobeying God, but had come to feel very sorry for all his wrongful behaviour. He explained that he had asked for his heavenly Father's forgiveness, and of course Mammy's, too. He then asked them to forgive him.

They were only too delighted to hear this and they responded with hugs and kisses. This made us both so happy and grateful to our faithful Father. What a gracious God we have! How merciful he is to us, his frail and failing servants!

John stopped being a missionary on furlough, got a job as a charge nurse in a local hospital and devoted himself completely to restoring our confidence in him as a father and husband. As soon as I was fit enough, I managed to get a job as well, and at the same hospital. This was so good for me! I began to heal in every way.

Life was very different for us – we were once again a normal, happy family. Joy and laughter filled our home and all our lives once more.

I need now to jump back seven years. In 1972, John and I had taken a holiday on our own in Cornwall. One day, we went to some event or other at a very large Methodist church – I forget what it was – and in the line of people waiting to get in there was a couple about our age who, we noted, were reading and chatting about a book by Arthur Blessitt, I think.

As we filed into the church, this couple were directed to go upstairs, and so were we. They sat at the front, so we went to sit next to them. 'Are you here on holiday?', we asked. 'Yes,' they said. 'Are you?' They told us that their names were Brian and Marjorie Nichols.

That was the beginning of what was to become a very important friendship. Like us, they were spending 10 days in Cornwall, so we arranged to meet up on other days. Naturally, we told them we had three children and were on our first furlough from Ecuador. At the end of the holiday, they invited us to stay in their home in Kent and to bring our children, too.

John and I went to their church, Hawkhurst Baptist,

on the Sunday and made friends with the minister. We
had a lovely time there and were asked to come back a
couple of months later to give a report to the church on
God's work in Ecuador. Brian and Marjorie themselves
became really committed to us as a family and to our
work as missionaries.

After we got back to Ecuador, we heard from the
church secretary that the fellowship wanted to know how
they could become more involved with what we were
doing. We suggested, among other things, that they could
provide Christian ministry tapes for us and books for our
children.

Brian and Marjorie were faithful to us in so many
delightful ways. In 1974, when I spent such a long time
in that hospital in Cambridge, they and others from their
church were wonderfully kind to me. Later, after my
doctors asked John to join me in England, the Nichols
offered us a holiday at their home and, with the doctors'
blessing, we went – and what a deep solace that holiday
was to us both!

In November 1978, another member of their church,
who was not a friend of ours but knew us as missionaries
the church supported, testified that as he was praying
one day he had had an overwhelming conviction that
God would use our family in Hawkhurst and that John
would be their next pastor – the church was then in an
interregnum. Brian and Marjorie reported this to us, but
John was then in rebellion and didn't want to know.

The Nichols wouldn't take 'no' for an answer, however.
At first, that only made John all the more intransigent;
but they persisted and finally, when they approached us
again in October 1979, we both listened.

We went down to Kent for a weekend, to meet first
the church leaders and then the whole fellowship. What
a super time we had there! Lots of things were discussed.
John wanted to know whether it would be a team ministry,

as he felt strongly that the minister should not run the church. Everything was ironed out and we came away quite impressed. We went home to pray and look for guidance.

On the way home, our children were so enthusiastic they said in unison: 'That's the sort of church we should be in!' John cautioned them and told them we 'must really seek what the Lord wants'. They agreed – but they were certain it would prove to be God's will!

We prayed hard. It would be a big thing to uproot our family again. John and I felt that we needed, as the Brethren say, to 'put out a fleece' (as Gideon did in Judges 6:33–40). We had tentatively said yes, we were interested in the offer; the 'fleece' was that we would know for sure that it was our Father's will for us if the fellowship was unanimously in favour of us coming. We did not want to go if anyone had reservations.

The secretary, a man called Walter Martin, rang the evening after the vote and (having no idea about our fleece) enthused: 'John, you and Brenda have made history in our church tonight: there was a unanimous decision you should come. This has never, ever happened before – and our fellowship's almost a hundred years old!'

John told him about our fleece and he was thrilled to have this amazing endorsement from God.

When we went to Hawkhurst again to visit the church, I was astonished to see the manse, which looked just like the doll's house I had seen in my mind's eye in Ecuador. I dragged John over the road to see it. 'This', I said excitedly, 'is the very picture of the house the Lord gave me in Santo Dom, when he told me I had to trust him with our family as he was going to use us for his glory. Do you remember me telling you how I dreaded us coming back to England – and of God's promise?'

'I do remember!', John exclaimed. 'Wow!' It was further confirmation that we were following the Lord's direction and, like me, he was exhilarated. This, on top of so many other signs, strengthened our confidence in God and filled our hearts with joy.

We moved to Hawkhurst in February 1980. Soon after we were settled into the manse, in April, John had to go back to Ecuador for a month. He had told the church that he would have to, as there were legalities regarding the house we owned outside Santo Dom that needed to be sorted out and his attempt to deal with them the previous year had been cut short by the car crash.

His schedule there was hectic and he had to deal also with some very delicate problems at El Buen Pastor, but it seemed that, through his own experience of alienation, the Lord had prepared him to handle them. What a gracious God we have!

Most people in Ecuador have a break from their jobs over Easter, which means that at that time of year the mail gets disrupted. Nonetheless, we wrote to each other often, hoping that some at least of our letters would get through. The first one I received from John was so encouraging to me! He wrote:

> Brenda, I miss you so much here, it's like an ache in my heart, I feel so very lonely without you. Darling, I'm longing for you. ... You become truly more precious and attractive to me – in fact, lovelier! I'm so proud of you, you satisfy me completely, in every way. You are the most precious human being on earth to me.
>
> I think I am the happiest man alive and thank the Lord that you are my wife, my best friend, the oneness we have is so amazing; also amazing is our Father's wonderful blessing! I am so humbled, and grateful to Him...
>
> Darling, I love you with all my heart.

Naturally, I wrote to him, too, before I had had anything from him. In one letter, I said:

John, I feel you are so near to me, I sense that you are thinking about me, loving me deeply!! It's the Lord's doing, praise His name, our spirits are reaching out to each other and somehow they touch and we are blessed and helped in our different circumstances.

People do say, and they may be right, that there is no truth that marriages are made in heaven, but I believe that ours was planned there!!

No two people could be more 'in love' than we are, after all that we have been through *together*, we are more 'in love' than ever. I see that God foreordained for us to be man and wife. The Evil One has attempted at least three times to make our union of no effect for God... We are both, of all people so unworthy, that's what makes it so amazing!! May we keep a humble spirit and recognise continually His amazing grace. It is late, but not too late to tell you, my handsome darling John, just how much I long for you and love you, it would be lovely to just snuggle up in bed with you right now and express all I feel for you, my sweetheart.

May you feel my love, across the miles, and God's wonderful blessings where you are...

When John got back from Ecuador, he needed a couple of days to recover from his travels, and for us to spend some time together. We planned a day out as soon as possible, when we made some sandwiches and a flask of hot coffee and went for a drive in the countryside.

At first, it was raining hard, but when it stopped we decided to park the car and go for a walk. The sun was shining and we saw a rainbow – a complete half circle! It was so beautiful, with all its colours so distinct, that it was like another encouraging sign from the Lord. Our first year back in England had been rather traumatic for us as a family; we had been humbled and now we felt very unworthy of this new opportunity to serve him.

A rainbow is a covenant sign of hope and grace and now it seemed to us like a benediction. We hugged each other so hard and were both so moved by wonder at God's amazing love and mercy that tears filled our eyes. We were forgiven and blessed.

The last two verses of Psalm 30 came to my mind and I repeated them to John:

> You turned my wailing into dancing;
>> you removed my sackcloth and clothed
>>> me with joy,
>> that my heart may sing your praises and
>>> not be silent.
>> LORD my God, I will praise you forever.

That was exactly how we felt!

We flourished in that church, and so did our children. There was no doubt in our minds that the comforting promise God had made to me before we returned to England was coming true. Moreover, the Lord's work in the area was really blessed by our family, and our home became a real refuge for so many people.

I shall never forget John's tender love during those early years in Hawkhurst. I was working three nights a week at the local cottage hospital and I have precious memories of his help around the house, doing the laundry, the hoovering and the washing up. He had always been a helpful person but he had never been domesticated before – he had never had to be.

He had a full life in the church, and was also studying at Spurgeon's College for a degree in theology. I used to listen to the same tapes that he had to listen to, and what companionship we had and how much I learnt! We grew closer and closer to the Lord and to each other as we heard God's voice in his word.

At John's induction, he told the congregation how in 1978 we had been given the prophecy by friends at the church, that we were to work there, but he had dismissed it. He had not wanted to listen back then – he was not interested in knowing God's will.

He explained how in June 1979 he had been called back from Ecuador, where he had gone to sort lots of things out, after his mother, his brother and I had been involved in a car crash. He said that this had confused him and only increased his rebellion, so that his heart was at war with the Spirit of God.

He recounted how God had dealt with us both: how he had been humbled and had come to repentance, and how the Lord had since worked in our lives in so many ways that we were now united in looking willingly for his direction once more.

He finished by telling the congregation: 'My challenge to you today is the same one Joshua put to the Israelites: If you are unwilling to serve the Lord, choose this day whom you will serve, whether the gods of your ancestors or the gods of the people you are living amongst; but as for me and my household, we will serve the Lord.'

And the people answered: 'We will serve the Lord!'

Chapter 18

The years John and I spent in Hawkhurst were some of the happiest of our lives together. The Lord blessed our work, and our family life was a joy.

John was much more involved with his children than at any time before. He had always been a loving father, but all too often in the past his time and attention had been devoted elsewhere. I have warm memories of the conversation and laughter that flowed around the table every day in the manse. John was the instigator of debate and really listened to his children.

The enthusiasm and concern he had for all of us were wonderful. We would put in our diaries weekends away, just to take stock of our relationships and express all that was on our minds and in our hearts. Those times were so precious, and our deep love and friendship continued to grow year by year.

We bought a little caravan with the insurance money from the car accident and what holidays we had in it! Later on, when our household grew larger, we would pack our tents and go on adventures together. And what fun John was on our holidays! I'll never forget his Ministry of Silly Walks along the beach in Eastbourne. He also organised a Valentine's disco in our home for our children and their friends from school.

John was often away, but he would write to his three children individually and kept in touch with me with loving phone calls and letters. Once, he wrote as follows:

> My darling, I didn't expect to get any mail, but I'm unable to cope with not having contact with you, it is extremely hard, I wish I could cope with it better. You are the only friend to whom I can really bare my heart and soul and share everything. I have absolute confidence

in you and in the light of all that we have been
through together I just know there can never
ever be anybody [else] like you in my world.
If I could have my life over again there are
certain things I would want to change, you bet
there are – but one thing is certain – if you
would still have me, my choice of wife, friend,
lover and mother of my children would be
the easiest in the world to make – YOU! AND –
please read carefully – there is nothing about
you I would want to change; I would want you
as you are. I love you with all my heart and
miss you like crazy!

Our reunions were always romantic, exciting and very
loving.

Whenever possible, John would drive over to collect me
from work after my night shift. The hospital was only a
20-minute walk away from our house, but he insisted
that it would give me a bit longer in bed.

I was always up by 3.30pm as I would have household
jobs to do, including an evening meal to cook. I always
welcomed the children home from school with tea and
biscuits and I listened to all their chatter. Sometimes I
would ask about any difficulties they were having.

It was after they started going to school in Kent that
our two daughters dropped the second half of their names.
In Ecuador, it was common for people to have double-
barrelled names, but now our girls were being teased for
being 'posh'! Henceforth, they decided, they were to be
simply Mary and Ana.

I recall Mary being very upset about a girl who was
bullied every single day on the bus to and from school.
She cried as she told John about it. He went and had a
chat with the headmaster and things did improve for that
poor girl. Mary never knew what her dad had done, but

she was so happy to tell him how things had changed!

When John realised that I was earning twice as much as him and it was going straight into our joint bank account, he said I must have some money of my own. He opened an account for me and showed me how to use it, and a small amount went into it for me to spend on clothes and footwear and other things I needed as a woman.

This was a new experience for me. I hadn't had any funds of my own since I was married, as John had always dealt with all our expenditure, even on household things, and I had very rarely asked for anything. I was very out of touch where money was concerned.

I now had the fun of buying clothes I really liked and having my hair cut professionally. For the first time since my wedding day, I was able to make myself look attractive. In charity shops, I found clothes that were both very stylish and affordable. John was amazed and delighted by my new persona!

In 1981, a Northern woman we had known years before rang to ask whether she could come and visit us. Her husband was a minister of a free church, I think, and when she arrived she told us that she was completely broken because she knew he was having an affair.

She said they needed help, and so it was agreed that the whole family should come down to Hawkhurst and we would see what could be done for them. The manse was a spacious place, with five large bedrooms, so it wasn't too difficult to fit everyone in when her husband and their two young children joined us.

He was deeply confused at first, and at times quite angry with his wife, which made the situation very distressing. He calmed down eventually, and softened, and then he was more contrite and wanted to listen and answer questions. It was such a humbling for him to cry and ask his wife to forgive him. Deep down, he didn't want to end his marriage or go with the other woman, and so we were able slowly to guide and help them through to real restitution and forgiveness.

They stayed with us for about three months. The man was able to find work and they ended up living in a neighbouring village. John saw them regularly for quite some time and they made a very good recovery. Both of them proved to be an invaluable asset to the church they now went to, and we were thrilled to see them go from strength to strength.

The woman is still a dear friend of mine; her husband died a few years ago.

The following year, my brother and his wife sold their house in Leeds and moved to one just up the road from us. They started coming to church with their children, Alison and Philip, and in time they all found the Lord.

Sadly, Maurice and Val had their own marital issues and less than two years later they separated, and later divorced.

My sister, too, had been having marital difficulties for some time and had often been on the phone to me. One evening in 1983, she called me in a dreadful state, begging us to come and get her and her daughter, Sharon. So, off we went.

When we got there, we found Marlene, who looked very ill, in emotional meltdown. Her husband was at work – he worked nights – so she simply packed a couple of cases of clothes and she and Sharon came back with us.

After four months or so, Marlene came downstairs one Sunday morning and announced: 'I'm coming to church this morning. I can't beat you all, so I've decided to join you.' Later that year, she accepted the Lord as her Saviour – and what an amazing transformation! From then on, she blossomed.

She and Sharon stayed with us for about eight months, until Marlene managed to get a cleaning job at the cottage hospital, when they moved out to a flat she rented.

Early in 1984, we were joined by a 17-year-old girl called Anna Lisa who was in desperate need of a home; and then, in the summer, after their parents separated, my niece and nephew, Ali and Phil, who were then 18 and 17. We were a big household for several years – there was a lot of coming and going, but at one stage, I remember, we had to turn the dining room into a bedroom for Mattie and Phil. I especially cherish my memories of our evening meals together.

Working the night shift at the hospital, I was often spending 12 hours at a stretch with the same colleagues, and naturally we talked about many things. My husband being a Baptist minister, it was inevitable that the subject of Christian belief would come up, and I was able to tell them my own testament of faith.

Some of these women were experiencing real problems in their marriages. I shared this with John and we began to pray for wisdom. After a while, we came up with the idea of doing 'couples encounter evenings', at which my nursing friends and their husbands would be joined by some couples from the church.

We set up round tables with an attractive tablecloth and a small vase of fresh flowers on each. John and our team of helpers really won our visitors' hearts, and each time they came they heard more about God's love and grace and what marriage was all about.

Some of my colleagues found the Lord and they and their husbands had in-depth counselling – and some of our church friends, too, recognised that they needed some 'orientation' in their marriages. At one time, I think, there were six couples or more receiving help. I remember John's humility and deep understanding in his whole-hearted commitment to this awful, painful problem in both the community and the church.

One of the nurses and her husband became an amazing asset to our church – she eventually became a deacon. (We had a wonderful group of deacons, who from the very start were a tremendous support and encouragement to John – and he in turn respected and listened to them. The church's ministry was very much a team effort.)

Like all fellowships, we had many deeply troubled people who needed pastoral care, and so a care group was set up, of which I was a member. If ever we found we were struggling, we would seek help from John; but the group member who had asked for help would always be present, as we dealt mainly with the women of the church.

Of course, there were difficult times. John and I were often deeply saddened by people's hidden sin and the bitterness and pain that were caused for so many by all the intrigue and deceit it involved.

There were two marriage breakdowns in the church and John and I were heartbroken as we witnessed the effects on the children of those broken relationships and the anguish of the people left to pick up the pieces.

John found many ways to reach the people of Hawkhurst. For example, we split into groups of four and, while two stayed in the church to pray, the other two would go out knocking on doors with a questionnaire. We would start by saying who we were and why we were calling: we wanted to know how the people in the village were and to invite them to try the church one Sunday. We ended by asking whether they would like an introduction to the Bible in their own home. A good number said yes.

In time, we visited every single house in the village. This outreach was blessed by God, and many people either came back to the Lord (and joined the church) or accepted Jesus for the first time as their Saviour.

We also had exciting evangelistic campaigns, with great results.

As the church's membership grew, the children's work, the youth work and the uniformed group called 'Campaigners' all grew as well. This was such a joy to the leadership of the church, and especially John. When he was alone with me, he would tell me how unworthy he felt and he often thanked me for being 'just right for me', his loving wife and co-worker and his very best friend.

A music group was formed – as was a choir, by our dear friend Trevor Golding. He and his wife, Lois, will always have a special place in my heart. They were a tremendous blessing to both us and the church. They led the youth group for some years and I know they have some happy memories of the antics of our three children.

A drama group was established, and in 1993 it performed in Folkestone at a national celebration by the Baptist Missionary Society of the 200th anniversary of the start of William Carey's work in India. My nephew, Phil, excelled himself – he played Carey!

We had a liturgical dance group, too, which became very expressive. John and I loved it, and he used it on very special occasions.

I could go on forever about our 13 years in Hawkhurst, it was such an amazingly blessed time. There was so much going on – and our fellowship grew and grew, until we had to extend the sanctuary.

John and I, too, continued to grow, in every area of our lives. We were full of gratitude to our heavenly Father for the overwhelming love, grace and mercy he showered on us, our children and (most importantly) his work in the church and the area.

Chapter 19

Let me say a bit more about my lovely children. All three of them came to faith when they were very young, and God has always been very real to them.

Naturally, there were times when they pushed the boundaries John and I set for them. They did disobey us sometimes, and they argued with each other and there were instances of bad temper and sulking. On the whole, though, they never caused us much anxiety, and most of the time they were a joy – and still are. They have been a tremendous encouragement to John and me, and to many others, too.

What an asset they have been in our service for the Lord! In Ecuador, they loved to help in any way they could. In Kent, they became very involved in the life of the church and were a real catalyst for the youth work. (When we moved to Hawkhurst, Mary was 15, Matthew was nearly 13 and and Ana was 11.)

They were always ready to make room for those in need. Our new home seemed to have elastic walls, but they loved this and often said that it reminded them of life in Ecuador.

All three of them have a compassionate heart and as adults they have all gone into caring jobs and have done well. Mary and Matthew both have a master's degree in some aspect of nursing, and Matthew also has a degree in applied theology after studying at Redcliffe College. Ana has a doctorate in psychotherapy; her speciality is grief, especially in children.

Ana was the first to get married, to Kevin Draper in 1988. Mary married Alan Digman the following year and Matthew married Tricia Waylan the year after that.

Some of the family have suffered ill health and gone through very difficult times. Both our daughters became type 1, insulin-dependent diabetics when young – Ana when she was just 13, Mary when she was 25 and pregnant with her first baby.

In 1990, Ana had to have huge surgery in London as she had an osteoma in the frontal part of her cranium, and it took her at least a year to recover from that. As usual, John was a tower of strength to all the family throughout her illness, and especially to Ana, Kevin and me.

Mary's husband, Alan, has twice had cancer, and he nearly died the second time after it got into his bones. In recent years, he has developed auto-immune problems that inflamed his pancreas and he, too, is now an insulin-dependent diabetic.

Two of my daughters' children, Alice and Sky, also became insulin-dependent diabetics while at university.

Matthew and his family enjoy good health, but at work he went through a long and painful ordeal in which his Christian stand took a battering. This took many months to resolve, but in the end it turned out to be a blessing.

The Lord entrusted six young lives to our care during our years in Hawkhurst, and he has been gracious to them all.

Phil, after getting married to Claudia, went to study at Spurgeon's like John and became a Baptist minister.

Ali and Anna Lisa, too, grew as Christians. Ali married Rob in the mid Nineties – they brought us back from Ecuador so that John could officiate at their wedding – and today she is a partner in an insurance business. Anna Lisa is now happily married to Tristan.

Ana and Kevin, Ali and Rob and Anna Lisa and Tristan all live in Hawkhurst and are all such good friends to me! Mary and Alan live in a village five minutes' drive away.

It was 1989 when, under emotional strain as a result of Ana's illness, I decided that I should take a break from the responsibility of being in charge of the hospital at night. After a few months, I managed to get an amazing job as one of the trained nurses at a home for female drug addicts and alcoholics, which was part run by nuns and part NHS.

The role of the SRN was to run the infirmary where the newcomers were detoxed from whatever it was they were addicted to. Some were very ill and in some danger – coming off either drugs or alcohol is very tricky.

These young women were at their lowest ebb when they came in and the care we nurses had to give them required real wisdom and lots of love and patience. I was not the only SRN there who was a Christian, and we were very much united in the work we did.

At a certain stage in their detox, the women were allowed to go out for a weekend, so I started to bring now one, now another home with me. They would come to church with us, too, and the Holy Spirit began to work in the lives of a number of them.

When our church had a live link from a Billy Graham crusade in '89, I asked permission for them to come and the nuns were only too pleased to allow it. Two of the women came to Christ as a result, and one of the nuns, who had herself become dependent on Valium, made a deeper commitment to him. Others followed. How delighted we all were!

I worked at the home for about four years in all and I loved my time there. When John and I had our valedictory service in 1993, many of the nuns came, which really cheered my heart.

John was going back to Ecuador from time to time to help the lay leadership in both El Buen Pastor and some of its daughter churches in Santo Dom. As the years went by, he became concerned at the lack of depth in the teaching, and some of the men who had been converted in the late Sixties or Seventies began to plead for us to return. They were only too aware of how much they needed to learn about the word of God and how to teach it themselves.

I could see the need, but by now I was approaching my

mid fifties and hoping soon to become a grandmother. Emotionally, I was very involved with my children and their new families, and so wanted to be a real, hands-on granny and see my grandchildren grow and develop. What confusion and turmoil I went through when John said he felt that the Lord was calling us to go back! Also, my lovely Ana, who had experienced so much ill health, was still having serious problems.

The patience and loving concern John demonstrated only made things harder in a way, because I naturally wanted to please him. However, I knew that if it was God's will he would make it obvious to me, too, and would help me to deal with the losses I would face.

Early in 1990, we both went to Ecuador – my first trip back since we had returned to England in 1978. Much had changed, but Santo Dom was still dirty, chaotic and full of violence. There was corruption everywhere.

The first thing we did was arrange a five-day holiday on the coast at Atacames. We were in the Hotel Arco Iris, which had been greatly modernised since we first stayed there 20 years before. This was better than a second honeymoon for us – and the name of the hotel reminded us of the rainbow we had seen 10 years earlier.

What an amazing holiday that was, strolling down Memory Lane and recalling so many lovely times when our children were little and played on the beach!

Seeing my dear Ecuadorian friends again was quite wonderful, too – after two days, it seemed as if we had never parted from them. Everyone was working hard to persuade me that we must go back for another few years. I was still very opposed to the idea, however – I just didn't believe that I could cope with being so far away from my children or deal with all the changes I would have to make at this stage in my life.

The following year, when we were back in England, all the local churches joined together to host another Billy

Graham live link. It was an amazing time and, among many others we had prayed for, one of my doctor friends came to know the Lord.

During one of the services leading up to the live link, my heavenly Father spoke to me personally. John was the main speaker and his message was inspired; I was broken completely and I surrendered everything to the Lord and begged him to forgive me for resisting his will. Deep down, I had known what it was!

I realised that it was his plan for our family, that he would bless us all and we would be close to each other in heart, mind and spirit if we all put our trust in Christ.

Our children were very supportive and encouraging, even though they didn't like the idea of us going back to Ecuador. They knew their dad well and thought he might overwork us both.

John was delighted, naturally. He said something to me which he repeated many times subsequently: 'With you, my darling, I flourish as a man and as a Christian. We have no need to fear what lies ahead because we will be doing our Father's will. He will be with us and will equip us to deal with the trials we face.'

In October 1993, my first grandchild, John, celebrated his first birthday – a lovely family occasion that was very precious to us. Someone took a photo of John and me in which my eyes are shut and I look as if I'm asleep. The reason was that I had worked for hours clearing out all the junk in the attic, which we had to leave empty. John looks – well, like the proud grandad he was!

We said our goodbyes. That year, we were completing 30 years of marriage, of knowing the Lord's amazing grace and blessing. The first 15 had seen some wilderness times, but now it was as if he was saying: 'I will repay you for the years the locusts have eaten' (Joel 2:25). How wonderful is the faithfulness of our triune God, a God of love and mercy!

At our valedictory service at Hawkhurst Baptist, some of our extended family – the five Harts, Ali, Phil and Anna Lisa – sang the Graham Kendrick hymn 'The Servant King' in four-part harmony, which Matthew had transposed for us. Our dear friend Victor Jack spoke.

At this stage, I must acknowledge the help we received from four dear couples in Hawkhurst who became such a support to us. Walter Martin, who had been the church secretary for some years, and his wife, Val, were a great encouragement.

Then there was Midge and Reg Angel – Reg came to the Lord during John's ministry – and Kath and Stan Acland, who were such stalwarts in the church.

Finally, there was Derek and Margaret Martin. Derek was a member of the diaconate and a man with a real evangelistic heart and vision, who was very influential in the Billy Graham live links. He was the chairman of a Christian trust which gave us a lot of support, even providing us with a lovely bungalow in Eastbourne where we lived from 2007 to 2018.

All four couples were, and are still, very dear friends. Each in their own way has blessed us and our ministry and I owe them all a great debt of love and gratitude. All of them at some stage came out to Ecuador and saw first-hand what God was doing through the work we were soon to undertake there.

I love this photo, taken in Hawkhurst in 1978, which speaks of the joy
and unity we were to experience there as a family.

Top: Visiting our dear friends Brian and Marjorie Nichols in 1979. I don't like beards, so John grew one just to tease me.

Above: 'The Manse gang': Philip, Mary, Matthew and Alison at the back, Anna Lisa and Ana in front

Left: On our 25th wedding anniversary, very happy with life

Nicely brushed up for Ana's wedding in 1988

Above: With our dear friends Joyce and Bruce Moore in 1993, when John and I were living in the shell of the CCLE lecture hall. The woman eating toast is the same visiting missionary as before!
Below: John and me with the founders of the CCLE – and their wives. Fausto is standing next to John; Orlando is on my right, and Enrique is two to his right.

163

Above: John preaching in a little church out in the sticks. Even in the rainforest, he was expected to wear a tie!
Below: In our new brick house in New Horizons in 1995. The huge pile of sucres was not worth very much at all…

Above: Some of the first houses built for Orphaids
Below: The lovely Dr Luz Celly Piamba Paz, director of Orphaids, with her husband and right hand, Dr Fabio

On our 40th wedding anniversary

Above: Our nine grandchildren singing at our golden wedding anniversary service
Below: Visiting Brendita, her husband, Jorge, and their three children on John's last visit to Ecuador in 2016

Left: John dancing with Alice in 2017. At this stage, he still remembered his children and grandchildren.
Below: Mary and Ana standing outside Escuela Juan Hart in 2020

Chapter 20

We returned to Santo Dom in October 1993. This time, we
went out with a new missionary society called Latin Link
and we had to go through a really tough selection process,
plus a separate, in-depth psychological assessment.

Comparing notes later, we found that we had both felt
that we had to be completely candid and we had spoken
of the times when we had seriously failed the Lord and
each other. We wanted there to be no secrets between us
and them.

We wondered whether that might shut the door to us –
and we were thrilled when we were accepted. It gave us a
deeper assurance that our going back was the Lord's will
for us and that our family would be blessed, too.

We had two weeks in the United States on our way there.
We had many American friends from our years in Ecuador
between 1967 and 1978 and we had kept in touch with
them and had previously visited them in the US, and they
us in England. It was fantastic to have fellowship with
them now.

Not that our stay in the US was altogether easy! Our
suitcases were stolen en route from one state to another
and we lost our passports and all our clothes and papers,
so we had to spend some time getting replacements.

We had a super time with the Kuhlmans, a wonderful
family whose friendship, forged in 1968–69 when they
were in Santo Dom on short-term mission, we had
maintained over the years. Dear Lottie had written to us
in great distress in 1979, just after John had gone back
to Ecuador to sort out the problems over our house. She
had received a new photo of us with our prayer letter and
had had a very strong sense that as a family we were in
serious danger.

We had not been in contact with her since we had seen

them a year earlier, and her letter filled me with awe as I, too, was gripped by fear, over John's behaviour. And then the car accident happened!

The next person on our itinerary was our beloved Dona Sensenig, who had cared for our children in 1974 when I was sick in England and John had to come at short notice to be with me. She has been a favourite aunty of theirs ever since (and is now a favourite of *their* children).

Dona was working with Mexican immigrants as a midwife and she introduced us to her good friend and colleague Vida. We taught her staff the Spanish chorus '*Más allá del sol*' ('Beyond the sun'), which became very popular. (In 2019, when Dona and Vida came to England for our granddaughter's wedding, Mary and I took them to see John in the nursing home. We sang that song to him and his face glowed with delight, and he even tried to join in!)

Next, we went to see David and Patty Kryder – David had been the headmaster of a bilingual high school in Cuenca that some of our Ecuadorian teens had attended when we were there. We travelled on to Dallas, to visit Bruce and Joyce Moore and some of their children. All their family are so very dear to us and what a great joy it was to see them again!

When we arrived in Ecuador, we were met by another dear friend, Yolanda, and her new husband, Patricio. We had known Yoli from her childhood – she came to faith through the Sunday school in Santo Dom and lived with us for a short time during her high-school years. They welcomed us to their home in Quito, just for a night as we were anxious to get down from the mountains the next day to find somewhere to stay in Santo Dom.

The bus ride down the next day was quite emotional. The Andes were as amazingly beautiful as ever and it made our hearts sing! In fact, we did sing 'How great Thou art' in Spanish – and when we got to the end we got an enthusiastic round of applause from the other people on the bus.

We prayed together all the rest of the way to Santo Dom, with a deep sense of gratitude and wonder at yet another adventure in our lives in the will of God.

Yes, there were some feelings of inadequacy and fear of the unknown, and a real sadness at leaving our children and little John, and all those dear friends we had said goodbye to at the church in Hawkhurst. We would miss the love and the security. Nevertheless, we knew that we were being obedient to God, the Lord of our lives, and he would never fail us. In his strength, we could continue to build up the church, as long as we made sure that we kept close to him and to each other.

A charitable trust that we knew based in Eastbourne had bought quite a large piece of land four miles or so from the centre of Santo Dom and donated it to a brand new organisation known as CCLE (or CLE for even shorter). The vision was to build a lecture hall, with some cabins for visiting church leaders, and to present weekends of in-depth teaching on the Bible, theology, sermon-writing and preaching style, and the importance of pastoral care. 'CCLE' stands for *Centro de Capacitación de Líderes Evangelicos* (that is, 'Training Centre for Evangelical Leaders').

A man called Steve Flashman had led a team from Soapbox Expeditions to start the building work in 1992. Our son, Matthew, and his new wife, Tricia, had been on that team, which even laid the foundations of what was to be our house.

When we arrived at the site, the shell of the lecture hall, where we were to live pro tem, was nearing completion. There were three very small rooms at one end of it; one was to be our bedroom, one became the kitchen and the third was a storeroom. The floor was still unfinished and its rough cement surface was very powdery, which was quite a problem for us – it got into our shoes, into our hair, up our noses, everywhere!

We assembled the bed we had bought on our first day, and made some furniture out of packing cases with the aid of our dearest Ecuadorian friends, Fausto and Maria, and their children. We rigged up a makeshift shower and toilet, just as the Villareals had as pioneer missionaries in the late 1930s. At the end of that day, we fell into bed somewhat shattered!

The next morning, very early, Fausto arrived with a lot of food – and a dog. He told us: 'I was so worried about how vulnerable you are here, so here is my lovely Kataplum.' (He had named him after a brand of chewing gum!) 'He is a very good guard dog,' he explained, 'so if he growls, be alert!' He also lent us a gun, 'not to shoot anybody, just to fire in the air, to let them know that you can defend yourselves.'

We were soon settled in. Some of our stuff had arrived before us, so we started to unpack our kitchen equipment. In the same box we found our tape recorder and some cassettes, mainly of Christian music plus some favourite classical albums, so we had the joy of listening to Verdi, Vivaldi and others.

We also had recordings of our valedictory service and of some of our family. It made us happy and sad at the same time to hear them when we were so far away from them and so many friends in and around Hawkhurst. (Wonderfully, we were able to contact our children once a month by telephone in the town. Eventually, they would come out to see us, which was always a joy.)

The next morning, a group of builders arrived, along with some other men who were going to dig a well before the rainy season really got underway. Some of them we had known back in 1967–71, and it was a real delight to learn that some of them who had become Christians then were still going on with God.

John and Fausto started directing the men. I got busy on the domestic front, as they would all be needing at least one big meal, as well as drinks and snacks through the course of the day.

Fausto and Maria were an amazing help. They often brought their family over in the evenings to give us some company. Sometimes their daughter Elisa stayed the night, so we cobbled together a bed for her in the store.

I think she must have been 10 or 11 years old at the time. I don't think I had met her before, but she has been such a dear friend ever since.

The first night she stayed with us, we put on some classical music, including a favourite of ours, 'The Four Seasons'. The inner walls of the rooms didn't meet the ceiling – they were only about seven foot high – so she could hear the music as if it were in her own room. She was still raving about it the next morning. It seems she had never heard orchestral music before and 'it sounded like music from heaven!', she exclaimed.

We got into a rhythm of work, John usually outside with the men and me acting as chief cook and washer-up. There was plenty for me to do keeping the whole place clean and the cooking and eating areas in particular sanitised, and making sure that all our water and salads were free from amoebas.

The well was finally dug and a pulley system installed. I could just about raise a bucketful of water, but John got a bit cross at me when I did, so if there were no workmen available he made sure that he did the hauling of water.

Actually, the well was not quite so essential during the rainy season, as we had plenty of water and to spare from the tin roof. (At night, it could be quite noisy – if it was raining hard, it was thunderous!)

John soldered a shower head into the bottom of a metal bucket and rigged it up on a pulley in the toilet so that we could take showers.

Some work was commenced on the main hall. The noise and vibration and dust proved to be quite tiring for us, but it had to be done so that John could soon start working in some way with the lay men of the churches.

Other people began coming in the evenings with Fausto and his family and we had some lovely times of worship together, also reminiscing about past adventures with lots of fun and laughter. Because our days were so busy, we actually ended up begging people to give us some evenings to ourselves!

Living like this, camp-style with no real privacy, was hard for both of us. We felt the need to have our devotions together – it was so important for us to be able to share with each other and have fellowship together, to tell each other what we were facing separately and even to receive comfort from each other.

Eventually, the main hall was finished and ready for what it was designed for. However, we still had to live there because our new house was far from ready.

The building was on a very gentle slope, with the space we occupied at the lower end, and one night it rained so hard that we awoke to find water flowing down the hall into our rooms. We ended up having to try to dig ditches around the front and sides of the hall so that the flood could drain away!

At one point, I looked over at John and the sight of him in boxer shorts and wellies seemed so comical to me, I couldn't help falling about with laughter. He didn't see what was so funny at first, which only made me laugh even more. He responded by shovelling up some mud and throwing it at me, hitting me in the midriff.

In the end, we were both laughing hilariously and having such fun together. All the while it was raining hard, so we had to get on with digging our ditches. Once they were deep enough to deal with the flood, we set to sorting out our bedroom and the other rooms.

We were both pouring with sweat and covered in mud by the time we were done, so we put a huge pan of water to heat on the Calorgas stove and eventually had a shower together under the bucket in the loo.

After that, we fell into bed again – but it was hard to get to sleep. John put his arms around me and said: 'I hope you're not regretting being here.'

'No, of course not,' I replied. 'We are right where we should be... But, I must say, with you, John Hart, life is never dull!' We started giggling about what we had just gone through. We did eventually get a couple of hours' sleep.

Two weeks later, as a result of the continual damp, both my Achilles tendons became inflamed and they remained so for quite some time. I couldn't walk properly and had to shuffle around. How the men teased me! They didn't know that it was a really painful condition – and it seemed to take forever to get better.

Chapter 21

John was seconded to CLE by Latin Link and was to devise and present a programme of teaching there for local lay pastors. The leaders of Santo Dom's evangelical churches wanted to get on with some weekend retreats and these started very soon after all the cabins were finished and the plumbing installed.

These were such a blessing to me as I was able to build up my friendships with the pastors' wives and children – the women looked to me for all sorts of advice. They were eager to learn all that their husbands were learning, so John allowed them to come to his lectures as well – which was very unusual for Santo Dom! We also started some separate Bible studies for the wives, who I was teaching to set up Sunday schools and do friendship evangelism.

The catering for the retreats was quite a big job, so I had to employ some of the women from the small nearby hamlet, which also proved to be another form of outreach for me locally.

Towards the end of the year, something happened that was very special to John and me.

During our first term in Ecuador, I had delivered many babies and quite a few had been named after me. I invited the parents of one of these to the church, and Bella and Manuel started to attend quite regularly.

When Brendita was a little over a year old, her mum ran away with some other man, leaving Manuel holding the baby. He had no relatives in the area and was at a loss to know what to do with her while he was at work. As a family, we felt that we should help by caring for her during the day.

After some time, Manuel got a new job that required him to travel and sometimes he would get home quite late... In the end, the little girl became a member of our family and we all grew to love her deeply.

What became of Brendita while we were absent from Santo Dom is a bit of a blur to me now, but certainly she was living with us when she was eight years old, when one day her mother turned up out of the blue and demanded her back. This was a shock to us all – our own children were really distressed about it, and John and I were both at a loss to know why Bella should want to take her back after all these years.

However, the law was on her side and we had no choice but to let her go. We subsequently lost all trace of them – though we never stopped looking. (Even after we returned to England, John would make enquiries whenever he was back in Ecuador.)

Two days after Christmas in 1993, it was raining thunderously when John shouted above the noise that there were some people at the gate and off he went with our big umbrella. I assumed it was some of the students, so I went to get some drinks ready.

I came back to the main hall to find a young couple and two small children, all dripping wet. The woman came shyly forward and, a little tearfully, asked me whether I remembered her. She looked at John, too, including him in the question. Neither of us could say yes, but I replied: 'You do look familiar... I feel I should know you...'

She came closer and, embracing me, said: 'I'm your Brendita and I've never forgotten you, Mamita, or you, Papito!' All four of us – her husband included – were so undone emotionally that we cried – really sobbing, very Latin! – from a mixture of joy and sorrow. It had been about 15 years since we last saw her.

They had been told we were back in Santo Dom by a half brother of hers who had been visiting the town. They lived on the Peruvian border, so they had sold a pig for the fare and travelled for 12 hours by bus to find us.

We made them comfortable for the night as best we could, and the next day John went into town with them and put them into a hotel for three days. We had a lot of catching up to do – Brendita wanted to know all about Mary Jane, Matthew and AnaMari.

Brendita and Jorge came to visit us many times after that, and continued to do so whenever we were in the country. John and I were adopted as grandparents to their children, and I am still very involved with them. Sadly, I have doubts as to where they are with the Lord, but I keep loving and praying.

After 10 months, we were able at long last to move into our new house, though it was still only part finished. The floors had yet to be laid and the plumbing was incomplete – we were still using the bucket-and-pulley shower and we had to flush the toilet with buckets of water.

We had a visitor that year from our church in Hawkhurst. Doreen was one of my nursing friends who had been converted in our third year there – I had given her and her husband, Richard, a copy of C S Lewis's book *Mere Christianity* and they asked so many questions after reading it and eventually came to know the Lord personally, which was a great joy to us.

They flourished as Christians and were faithful to the Lord in all their ways and became well loved in the fellowship. When Richard was diagnosed with inoperable cancer at the age of 62, we were all deeply affected. As he was nearing his end, very frail, John and I would visit him daily. He was only 64 when he died; Doreen was just short of 60.

Doreen came out to Santo Dom in September and so it was the dry season. No rains meant more work for us, carrying lots of buckets of water from the well a few metres from the house, and she always pitched in. What a joy she was to us, and such an encouragement! She stayed for a month and really enjoyed her time with us.

One day, John was showing a flooring contractor around

the house. As soon as he saw me, the young man stopped and stared. 'Is your name Brenda?,' he asked. Rather puzzled, I said: 'Yes. How do you know?'

'Many years ago, when I was nine or 10, you saved my life,' he replied. 'I could never forget your face or your name.'

John invited him to sit down and tell us the whole tale.

'I was very, very sick,' he began. 'My mother had heard about you folks and it was well known that the *gringuitos*' – an affectionate term for foreigners – 'would help us.

'When we got there, only the lady' – he meant me – 'was there. She said I was very sick with parasites, so she gave me some medicine and told me and Mother to wait in a little room with a bucket. I was very weak, so she took off my boots and put me on a bed and told my mother she would be in and out to see how I was.

'After half an hour or so, when nothing had happened, she brought in a strange-looking chair with a hole in the seat and a bucket fixed under it.

'It was not long after that that I started to vomit huge worms – thick ones and thin ones. I started to choke and Mother ran outside calling to Brenda and she came and got a hold of me round the middle and banged my back. I stopped choking, but I still was vomiting lots of worms. Then I needed the toilet, so I was passing worms, both ways, for quite some time.

'All this time, Brenda was reassuring me. Gradually, things calmed down, but I felt faint and I was unable to stand. I think I did faint, because when I came to I was in the bed, feeling very ill.'

The young man, whose name was Juan, continued: 'When John saw me later, he said I would need to go to hospital as I was so anaemic. My mother started to cry: "How can I take him to Quito? I have no money."'

By this point, I had remembered the whole story. John and I had felt that this boy's health was so poor that he needed urgent treatment, including blood transfusions, so we decided that I would take him to the mission hospital in Quito on the morning bus. John had some important appointments that day that he could not cancel.

I was about five months pregnant with AnaMari, I think, and I was nervous about taking such a sick child on a three-hour bus journey; but John and I prayed just before Juan and I left and we put all our trust in the Lord. In fact, we made it to Quito without too much trouble, but Juan was so weak I had difficulty getting him off the bus at the other end.

The driver was very kind and called a taxi, which took us straight to the hospital. Juan was seen by a doctor very quickly, who said he was near collapse and needed a transfusion as soon as they knew his blood group. I was with Juan the whole time and I lost count of how much they gave him in the end.

John came up the next day, so that I could get home to the children and rest – I was feeling worn out by the time he arrived. All ended well. I was able to follow up Juan and his family and they came to the clinic once a month so that I could keep an eye on them.

One concern we had was how we were going to pay the hospital bill. A collection was taken up at El Buen Pastor and, though it didn't quite cover everything, it was a big help.

Juan then told us: 'I now have my own business, so I will do your floor free – and it will be beautiful.' He was true to his word and we ended up with the loveliest floor, which had squares of marble set into it!

Doreen had been in the room all that time, listening to Juan's story (which a missionary friend who was staying with us was able to translate for her), and she was very moved by it. Seeing missionary work up close was a real eye-opener, she said, and she had lots to tell the church when she got home.

It was nearly Christmas by the time our house was ready. We had been back in Ecuador a little over a year and it was amazing how much had happened. We felt so grateful that we decided to have a little celebration at our home. We invited people from the adjacent hamlet – the area was still very rural, so there were not many of them – as well as the students and their wives and children plus our longstanding friends and their families, too.

The house overflowed with people. We sang our heart-felt praises and there was great thanksgiving for the way the Lord had blessed us all. We felt very encouraged to look forward with great anticipation to all that God had – and still has – in store for us.

The teaching of lay pastors had commenced quite early in 1994, and growing numbers were now following the curriculum John had developed. Their enthusiasm was very encouraging, but the wide range of ability and gifting was a problem. Also, John was concerned that some of the men were not really up to the job.

The love, sensitivity and wisdom required of him were enormous, and the way he managed those first three years was a testament to his faith, his trust in the Lord and his pastoral gifts. His success in teaching men who had had very little formal education was amazing. Those who did complete the full three-year course were trophies of our Father's love. Some of the more able academically became really good teachers themselves and would go on to help John teaching other students.

John saw through three sets of students. Eventually, in the late Nineties, a young English missionary called Tim Pawson took over from him, as we needed to get more involved in the start of the work of Orphaids.

A number of John's students who went on to be full-time pastors never forgot 'Juanito' and whenever he was in Ecuador thereafter, up until 2016, they made sure they saw him.

I don't remember when Orlando Castro came to CLE, or why. He was a Bolivian who had originally been working in a flourishing church in Machachi, a little to the south of Quito. (The pastor there was our good friend Enrique, who had previously run El Buen Pastor for some years with John.)

Orlando became a real asset to our team. He taught the guitar and keyboard, and showed music groups how to use their skills better and how to lead worship. A lot of people were helped by him.

About a year after he joined us, a lovely young woman called Sally-Anne came out from England with Latin Link. After a while, Orlando started taking an interest in her, and eventually they married and became full-time missionaries in Ecuador. To start with, they set up home in two of the CLE cabins, but in due course they bought some land and built their own house there.

Rather charmingly, the hamlet adjacent to CLE was called Nuevos Horizontes (or 'New Horizons'). Initially it consisted of just a handful of houses, but it rapidly grew into a substantial village. Orlando later developed an interest in piping water down to it from a small river further up in the mountains – I think I'm right in saying, with the help of his father-in-law, Fred.

Fred and Mary Kerridge moved out to Ecuador to live in a flat over their daughter and son-in-law's house. They became a real asset to New Horizons, where they did some splendid work, both practical and spiritual. We were blessed by them, as I know other missionaries have been.

Orlando and Sally-Anne now have two daughters, Dañela and Debbie, and live in Diss, in Norfolk, having moved to England for the sake of the girls' higher education.

Chapter 22

Alongside all we were doing in the teaching centre, other work arose from us just showing compassion, to the very poor, the sick and the vulnerable.

A very young couple came to tell us that they were greatly concerned for their three-year-old daughter and to beg us to visit them in their home. They lived way out in the sticks, so the girl's father, Roberto, came out of the forest to meet us. We had been walking for at least two hours and I was tired. I asked, 'How much further?' and he said: 'We just have to cross a river and then we are there.'

Not long after, we arrived at a fairly fast-flowing river, which we had to cross on some wobbly stones. Roberto went first, then me and then John. We had almost got to the other side when I missed my footing and fell in! It was only thanks to John's quick reaction that I was not swept downstream.

When we got to the house, I was given a skirt to wear. It belonged to Roberto's wife and on me it was more like a miniskirt!

It was obvious to us that the little girl (who was called Karen) was profoundly deaf. This encounter prompted us to start a work testing the hearing of the first-year children at the local schools, as there was a large number of deaf children in the area. We looked into why this might be and found that, while pregnant, women were often given lots of antibiotics in high doses for very trivial reasons.

We then noticed that many of the children had dental problems. I pointed this out to John and we started some classes on 'keeping your teeth clean' and dished out toothbrushes.

One day, I remarked to John that most of the parents also had really bad teeth. It must have stuck in his mind, because he later mentioned it to a Christian he met at some function in Quito who was training to be a dentist.

It turned out that in Ecuador dentistry students had to complete a three-year university course and then do a year of practice in the countryside. The man, who was called Mauricio, asked whether he could come and take a look. So he did – and decided that he would love to spend his practice year in New Horizons. It proved to be an amazing success. We became lifelong friends with him and later went to his wedding.

When his year was almost over, he told John of a student friend of his who needed to do a practice year and might succeed him. He told us: 'Elsa is a fine woman, very honest and hard-working; but she's not a church person. Would that put you off her?'

We accepted Mauricio's recommendation; Elsa came to look around and duly took the job. She was a really winsome girl, great fun and with a lovely personality. We got to know her well as she ate with us, and she started to come to the church services John conducted in the village.

As we grew closer, she began to talk to me about her family in Quito. She had many brothers and sisters; her parents were devoted to them all and her siblings, who were all quite ambitious, looked out for each other.

After a few months with us, she went home for a short break – and that weekend was involved in a car accident. She wasn't seriously injured but was rather shaken, so John advised her to stay at home and recuperate. When she rang us again a few days later, she was very tearful, so I offered to go to see her and we met for a cup of coffee in the shopping mall in Tahuaico, halfway between Quito and Santo Dom.

She confided in me that she felt God was speaking to her. 'I know I am far from being perfect,' she said, 'but I've always seen myself as a good person – until recently.' With this, she began to cry. I took hold of her hand and asked: 'Is it since your accident that you've been having these doubts?' She nodded, and said: 'It's also what I've been hearing from you and John, and what the Bible says. How do I make things right with God?'

I asked her whether she had ever seen that beautiful picture of Jesus standing outside a door. He has a lamp in his hand and is knocking – there is no way to open that door except from the inside! She answered: 'Yes, I know that picture. I've wondered what it means.'

'That door is the door to your heart, Elsa,' I said. 'Jesus is asking you to let him in. Only you can let him in, into the seat of your emotions and your will; but then he will do the rest. He wants to cleanse you,' I continued. 'He wants you to surrender all that you are – a woman, a daughter, a sister, a dentist – and all your desires. He must come first in your life, as your Saviour, your Lord and your Master. You know that he died for you.'

We parted with a big hug and she said she would be back in Santo Dom very soon.

She returned just a few days later, looking so excited and radiant. 'I've done it!,' she told me. 'I'm now a child of God! I've told my parents and some of my sisters, and they want me to tell them more next time I'm home.'

A few months later, Elsa's parents came to the Lord. She was a great witness to all her family, and in time many of her siblings also came to know the Lord.

When her practice year came to an end, she decided to stay on with us – and how fantastic she was at her job, and how fast she was growing as a Christian! It was no surprise to us that Tim Pawson (who had begun the process of taking over from John at CLE) fell in love with this lovely woman. A few years later, John was to officiate at their wedding in Quito.

They have been faithful servants of the Lord. They came to England in the summer of 2013 so that they could get a good high-school education for their daughter, a beautiful girl named Franchesca.

Sadly, a year and a half later, aged only 12, Franchesca became very sick and died quite suddenly from sepsis and organ failure. Her parents, and all of us who know and love them and all their family, are still grieving at this dreadful loss.

Tim and Elsa now live in Derby, with their son, Felipe. Elsa works in the Spanish department of the school where Franchesca was a pupil and she is so very appreciated. Tim works full-time doing Christian work in the local schools with Derby City Mission. I have stayed in regular touch with them, and they are an amazing testimony to God's love and care.

I must at this point introduce Cristina, who was a contact from the dental clinic. She was a woman in her late thirties who lived in a tiny hamlet not far from New Horizons. Her father carried her into the clinic wrapped in a sheet and, as soon as I saw her, it was obvious to me that she had rheumatoid arthritis, and must have had it since childhood. She was fearfully disabled, with twisted limbs and a twisted spine. She also now had a raging toothache.

Elsa and I laid her on the sofa we had in the waiting room. After a quick examination, Elsa said that Cristina had an abscess and would need antibiotics for at least a week. She would not treat her with an infection, so her father carried her away with some pills for the pain and said he would bring her back in due course.

As they were leaving, Elsa asked them where they lived, as she thought that maybe one of us should go and see how Cristina was responding to treatment. She told me afterwards that she was a little worried about the strength of the painkillers she had given her, as she was so frail.

I told John what had happened and we decided to go and see her in two days' time. In fact, it was three days later that we went to visit her, and what we found was shocking. Cristina and her father were renting a single room which was infested with cockroaches. They had no beds, or any furniture at all except a kerosene stove to cook on – they slept on two rush mats on the concrete floor. It was really awful!

Cristina's abscess was going down but she was still in pain, so John increased the dose of painkillers. We learnt that she and her father, who was called Jesús, had been Christians for many years but had only a limited understanding of the scriptures.

(I must admit that I found it quite hard to address someone as 'Jesus'. It's not an uncommon name in Ecuador and I did get used to it in the end!)

When we got back to CLE, we sought permission from some of the trustees to use one of the cabins to house Cristina and Jesús. We told them of their situation and they agreed that these two poor people should be helped.

The next day, we went and fetched them. They were so grateful! They had very little money – Jesús did what work he could get in the fields – so John said we would pay him to sort out the grounds and there would be no charge for the cabin.

Jesús and Cristina felt that some other member of the family should come and help with her care, and it turned out that she had a deaf-and-dumb niece, named Lupita, who was happy to join them. We gave Jesús further jobs in the grounds so that he could earn enough to keep them.

So it was that the three of them became part of the CLE community. Cristina was given a wheelchair by a short-term missionary, and she and her father came to our worship services and really blossomed, both as people and as Christians.

The last I heard of them, Jesús has died but Lupita is still caring for Cristina.

Life was always interesting for all of us who worked in CLE. Latin Link was a great mission to work for and we soon had news that a new venture was in the pipeline. Some short-term-service (or 'Step') teams were coming out to various parts of Ecuador to do something practical to help the people. They would arrive in July and stay until the end of August and would assist in constructing a building for a school or a church, or even a clinic.

Those teams achieved a lot, while they themselves had a cultural and spiritual adventure. John and I had to organise things in our area, taking care of the teams and overseeing their endeavours. It was a lot of work for us both while it lasted. A few of the young people from that time – now married with children – still keep in touch with me.

There was another Latin Link programme, called 'Stride', which brought young men and women to Ecuador for between three months and a year. Two of them came to Santo Dom.

Jonathan and Nathan arrived together and initially lived on the CLE site, I think, until we were able to place them in an Ecuadorian home. They had come for a year, Jonathan from Lancashire and Nathan from somewhere in the south of England, having both just graduated. What fun those two fellows were! Jonathan was to become a lifelong friend.

Both of them were only too willing to help in any way, so first they got involved delivering and collecting mail for a Step team we had way out in the sticks, which was building a small church and starting work on a primary school as well. (The school was later named Escuela Juan Hart!)

After two months, we managed to get a placement for Jonathan with Fausto and Maria. He really bonded with the whole family, and his Spanish got better and better.

When it was time for them to leave us, it was really hard to say goodbye at the airport. Jonathan vowed that once he had finished a year of teacher training and done a few months' teaching he would be back.

Nathan had fallen in love with one of the girls on the Step team and they eventually got married. She is a twin, and she and Nathan now have two sets of twins!

True to his word, Jonathan returned and he secured a post teaching English in Quito. By this time, Fausto and Maria's daughter Elisa was at university there – and the next thing we knew, Jonathan had asked her out. She could hardly believe it – she must have been 15 or 16 when he left for England and she said he had treated her as a little kid when he lived with her family. Now she was all grown up, a sweet and loving girl and a really lovely Christian.

They are now married and live in Preston, with two young children, Sofia and Lukas. They make time to visit Elisa's family in Ecuador and hope some day to return there to serve the Lord full-time as missionaries.

Jonathan and Nathan have always said that their year in Ecuador was an amazing experience for them – and I believe it was for John and me, too, we so enjoyed their stay!

We had a much less happy experience one year, just before Christmas. We were trying to make up lots of gift packages for the people who lived nearby. Most of these families were quite large and many were very poor, so we thought we would give each one some staple foodstuffs and, for their children, a toy and some things for school. We had a young short-term worker staying with us for a few days – his name eludes me, so I shall call him Martin – and he helped us. We had such fun doing it!

John had had a very stressful day, having had to rush into town for an important meeting. On his way home, he had called in at the bank to draw out a large amount of money. After we had had tea, he said he felt really unwell and went to lie down. I looked in on him an hour or so later and he was in a deep sleep.

Around 7pm, I decided to take a shower, perhaps with a view to getting an early night myself. Martin was at work on the computer when he heard someone banging on the main gate and went to see who it was.

There were three men outside, who said they needed to see John Hart urgently. Martin unlocked the gate and let them in. Just as he brought them into the house, I entered the sitting room to see three total strangers. Two of them came forward and took hold of me quite roughly, while the third produced a pistol and seized Martin. 'This is a hold-up,' one of them said. 'Where is John Hart?'

I called out to the Lord to help me to be brave, and told the men: 'My husband is quite sick at the moment and is asleep in bed.' Their leader said: 'Take me to him!' In that moment, I prayed for John. One of the men stayed with Martin and the other two went with me to the bedroom. John was still fast asleep and was shocked to be rudely awakened with a gun in his face.

He sat up in bed and the leader of the robbers said: 'We know you have taken a lot of money from the bank today, and we want it or you and your wife and son will die.' (They assumed that Martin was our son.) John got the money and gave it to them – he was so calm! – and said quietly: 'Now please go, and may God forgive you!'

The leader of the robbers said they hadn't finished yet. John, Martin and I were put in our bedroom with the man with the pistol and for about three hours the other two ransacked the house for anything they could find of value. That included all the Christmas packages we had made up for the locals.

Our bedroom was the last room to be searched. The men took my rings as well as a gold-plated watch that the fellowship at Hawkhurst Baptist had given me – things that were of great sentimental value. Martin was trembling, poor lad, while I was crying and shouting, venting my fury in English.

John put his arms around me and murmured: 'Calm

down, my love! The most precious things we have they can't take unless they kill us. I can't bear the thought of losing you, or this young man here.' I pulled Martin down onto the bed with us and we prayed in whispers that we would be kept safe.

It seemed a very long time before the robbers decided they had all they wanted. After they'd gone, I said: 'I need a cup of tea!' 'So do I!', chorused the others. How English was that?

We all needed to relax and take stock. The first thing we did was praise and thank our heavenly Father for keeping us safe. John's lovely prayer will always stay with me. He said: 'You, Lord, had given what was taken from us this night, and you have allowed it to be taken from us. Blessed be your name!'

I recognised that this was what Job had said after he had lost far more than we had. That prayer of John's humbled me and made me see that any treasure, even symbols with sentimental value, must be held lightly. My lovely John was such a gentle person! His quiet strength has been such a powerful influence on my life; his intimate relationship with Christ permeated his whole demeanour.

The young lad, Martin, suffered post-traumatic stress for a while and had to stay with us longer than planned, although he recovered before he left us. I feel so ashamed of the way I behaved in front of him – and that for the life of me I can't remember his real name!

Chapter 23

In 1996, I received a call from an American nurse who was managing a big TB clinic at the mission hospital in Quito. Her father was very sick and she had to go home at short notice, but it was imperative that the clinic should be kept open. Could I relieve her?

The clinic's concern with TB was genuine, but was also a cover for helping people with Aids. People who had this disease were at risk of being attacked and even killed, and those who wanted to help them had to do it discreetly.

After making sure that things in New Horizons could tick over for a few months without me, and inviting prayer for both me and John, I went up to Quito. What an eye-opener this experience was to be for me! It presented a huge challenge and changed my life.

The American doctor in charge – in England, we would call him a consultant – must have been a chest specialist. He was very grateful that I had come to help. He was a real gentleman, very approachable, and we formed a very good relationship. Although I worked with him week in, week out, his name now escapes me, though I remember it sounded foreign and was very difficult to pronounce. I always just addressed him as 'Doctor', which amused him no end!

First, he had wanted to know what I knew about HIV and was quite impressed when I told him. Fortunately for me, my son had taught us all a great deal about Aids.

Matthew had trained as a nurse and had gone on to specialise in palliative care, which required several years of study. He did some of this at St Christopher's, the pioneering hospice in south-east London founded by Cicely Saunders, a wonderful Christian woman who was made a Dame in 1979. The Aids epidemic was in full flood at the time, so Matthew had studied that, too, and he had nursed a number of dying young men at the Mildmay

Mission Hospital in the East End.

The men who came to the clinic in Quito were very young and very frightened. A few of them were members of the city's gay community. We also had very young women, too; some had been infected by their husbands, some were sex workers.

There was no treatment in those days, but we did know the difference in prognosis between being HIV-positive and having full-blown Aids. Aids patients suffered infections – principally TB, which eventually spread throughout their bodies.

Much of our work consisted of befriending fearful people and treating what we could. They really needed a lot of love. I cared for a number of young men and women in their pain, desperation and loneliness. I saw some of them come to Christ. I was with some of them when they died.

Some of the young women endured a double agony because they had small children. By the time we saw them, their men had already died. Sadly, their families were so afraid of the disease they abandoned them.

One girl who came to faith I shall call 'Monica'. I was very involved with her and cared for her through to the end, when she begged me to look after her two little daughters. I wrestled with the implications of that – I would be 60 in just over a year!

All of this had a profound effect on me. When Betty the nurse came back from America after two months away, she and I talked at length about all the children being orphaned by Aids. So many ended up living on the streets, surviving as best they could.

Betty brought it to the attention of the government, but nothing came of that. We said goodbye with sad hearts. Monica was dead and Betty found temporary care for her two little ones.

However, the Lord was not finished with this problem, or

with me, either. I told John all that was in my heart, things that had been oppressing me for months, which I could not let go. He and I were due for furlough in early 1997, so we decided to pray about how we should respond and what we should share with our supporters in England. We would give them some idea of what could be done and see what the Lord came up with!

The CLE team were very supportive when we told them, and were even excited by the thought of what might happen in God's will. CLE had plenty of land and they set aside what they thought we might need if we had to put up new buildings. We left for England feeling encouraged that the Lord was leading us to share our concern and our vision there.

In fact, there proved to be far more interest in England than we had expected. The consensus was that we should go ahead, and we raised enough money to build four houses.

Soon after we arrived back in Ecuador, we got a phone call from a member of the government of Jersey in the Channel Islands. We had been invited to speak at this woman's church by a couple we knew very well who went there, who John had helped earlier when they lived in Hawkhurst and were experiencing great stress in their family life.

Now the Jersey government wanted to send a team of professional builders and unskilled volunteers out to help us for a month – and possibly do more thereafter. In fact, they were to do an amazing amount over a number of years.

One volunteer from that church in Jersey, a vibrant young Christian called Nickie, was a GP. She came out as a missionary with Latin Link and started a hospice in Quito, where she met and eventually married a young dentist called Renaldo, who had worked for us in CLE.

After a year of building, we had two houses ready for occupation and a couple lined up to be our first houseparents. Mariana's two little girls were the very first children to come, and what was lovely, they remembered me. How wonderful is our heavenly Father!

The Jersey government subsequently provided the funds for volunteers from the church to build a block of flats to house sick mothers and their children, so that families could stay together right to the end – which in some cases was up to a year. We felt it was right that these children should be told the truth and should receive as much help as possible from a Christian psychologist – besides lots of love from the rest of us.

The name that John came up with for this work was 'OrphAids' ('Orphans due to Aids'), which in due course became 'Orphaids'. We felt strongly that the Ecuadorians should own it, so we set up a registered charity there; but we also had to register a second charity in the United Kingdom, to allow further financial contributions from there.

At the time of writing, Ecuadorian Christians are helping to raise a good amount of funds, and I am hopeful that some day soon Orphaids will no longer need foreign help.

While we were in England on furlough, we naturally spent time with our children and their babies. We had a reunion in a lovely house they rented in a very pretty village somewhere. What a super time it was for us, getting to know new grandchildren, going for walks in the beautiful countryside and sharing deeply with our children – not least, our new vision!

They were very interested and wanted to help in any way they could. In particular, Matthew and Tricia, when we were alone with them on another occasion, said they were very excited. They had been looking into becoming missionaries themselves, though it seems Matthew had been resisting the idea of going to Ecuador because his dad was there.

Now, though, they felt sure they could work alongside us, tackling the Aids epidemic and caring for people in Orphaids. Matthew had a real concern for prevention through education, as well as for reaching and supporting people with HIV in the community and showing God's love for them. His idea was to go into high schools and universities and organisations like the fire brigade, the army and the police.

We were very impressed with all he and Tricia said, so we pointed them to Latin Link. Three years later, in September 2000, they joined us at CLE.

What a joy that would prove to be, to work with our own son and daughter-in-law; and how gracious of God to let me be the hands-on grandmother I had always wanted to be! They had three little boys: James was five when they arrived, Peter was three, and Jonathan was almost a year old. They had their own house there, very near to ours.

They said they could give Orphaids five years, as Tricia was willing to home-school the boys until James was ready for high school. The four of us were to work together for three years.

Matthew and Tricia were an immense help in the work – what they achieved was amazing and it still continues today. I must say that Tricia was the most wonderful mother and teacher to her children; my admiration for her only grew as I got to know her better. We were very good friends and she gave me lots of time with the little ones, who loved to visit 'B' and 'Grandpops' most days.

In 2000, I returned to England to see a specialist about my hearing. I had had an infection in both ears which had ruptured my ear drums, and as John was going back to speak at some big function we decided that I should go with him. I had several appointments with an audiologist called Carol Gupwell, who sorted me out with my first digital hearing aids.

She and I took to each other immediately and she was interested in what John and I were doing in Ecuador. I told her about the problems the children of New Horizons had with deafness and she seemed very affected. 'I've always wanted to go somewhere where little ones are so disabled,' she said wistfully.

'Why not come out and help us?', I cried. 'We so need help to test the children properly! You could even train up an Ecuadorian to do the tests and then we'd be able to carry on the work after you'd gone home.'

To cut a long story short, she came out the following year, right at the end of the rainy season. It was only then that I discovered what a lovely Christian she was!

We sent word around all the local schools and started with the six- and seven-year-olds. With those in the immediate area, everything was easy. We found that a number had impaired hearing, so Carol fitted them with analogue hearing aids and batteries that she had brought from England.

The look of immense surprise that came over the faces of those dear little ones who had never heard clearly before delighted us all. The teachers were thrilled, and Carol was over the moon!

We then moved on to the outlying schools – John took us on dirt roads out into the sticks in a four-wheel-drive truck. On the first really muddy road, we got stuck and Carol and I had to give the vehicle a push while the back wheels spun and covered us with mud from head to toe!

When we got to the little school, the teacher and the children were astonished to see *gringos* so dirty. It was hilarious! After that, we found that we had to clean up when we arrived at each school.

What a sport Carol was the whole time she was with us! She also started to train up a very dear Ecuadorian friend of mine called Magali, a lovely girl who had started helping me back in 1994. She was a devout Catholic who had 'found the Lord' as we studied the Bible together.

Carol grew to love Magali as much as I did and for several years since she has gone back to Ecuador to further the work with her. They have rented a room in the CLE clinic where the children could be checked and their hearing aids cleaned and repaired (and, if necessary, changed).

Carol lives in Maidstone and is such a great friend. Sadly, I haven't seen her for ages, but we do talk on the phone.

On that same visit to England, a woman called Kate Henry, who lives not far from Hawkhurst, had spoken to John after a talk he had given about our work in Ecuador. She had just retired as a teacher for the deaf and was interested in doing something in the developing world, so he invited her to come out and see what we had in hand. He had mentioned in his talk that there was the beginnings of a school for the deaf in Santo Dom, the very first in that city!

She finally came out in 2002 for a three-week lookaround and felt sure that she could really be useful, both in the school and to Magali, too. She returned the following year as a missionary with Latin Link.

What an amazing help she has proved to be, in the work of the school and in all our ventures into the world of the deaf in the area! And what a terrific, loving friend to John and me, Magali and Carol! She joined us in funding Magali to go to the Catholic University in Santo Dom to study English, which gave her access to so much information on so many subjects. Magali was also able thereafter to teach English and so support herself and her family.

Jill Ball was someone else we met on that visit to England. She, too, had recently retired and was wondering what she could do with the rest of her life. She came out to see our work in Orphaids but quite quickly realised that the Lord was leading her to work with disabled people in the area, for whom there was no provision at all.

She eventually returned to Ecuador as a missionary with the South American Mission Society (Sams), a sending society of the Church of England which has since merged with CMS. She now has a wonderful charity called Life in Abundance, which is doing very well. She, too, has become a treasured friend. She, Carol and Kate have rented a flat together when all three have been in Santo Dom.

Two things happened around that time that affected John and me deeply. In 2001, Marlene suffered a cerebral aneurysm and was very sick, so it was arranged for me to go home. When I saw her in the hospital, she was in a coma. Sharon, my niece, told me the prognosis was that she could not recover from the damage to her brain.

I decided to stay a while to give moral support to Sharon and her children. After six weeks or so, Marlene was moved to a cottage hospital that was much nearer to all the family. It all seemed so unreal to me, that my lovely sister was dying – she was 62, only 15 months younger than me, and she looked so young. As I sat by her bedside day after day, I grieved deeply. What a wonderful mother and grandmother she had been, and the best of sisters!

My childhood and youth came flashing back to me: we had such fun together as kids, and she was always an encouragement to me in my teens and twenties. I have the loveliest of memories of her – even when life was tough for us growing up, we always saw the funny side of things!

Sadly, I needed to get back to John in New Horizons. Marlene died three or four weeks later, but I knew she was in the best place, close to the Saviour she had grown to adore. My prayers were for her children and grandchildren, who she had loved so much and who had loved her immensely.

In 2002, John and I returned to England on home assignment. His nephew, Andrew, the son of his brother David, was to be married that year to Stella, a young teacher who went to their church. How pleased we were to attend their wedding!

David had suffered heart failure and when we saw him we were shocked to see how far his illness had progressed. Later that day, as we were going, he came out to talk to us and say goodbye because we were to leave England the following week. He gave us a big hug and told us that he didn't think he had much time left and wanted to say that he would see us next in glory! All three of us were in tears as we hugged him again.

We had been back in Ecuador just over a week when David's wife, Brenda, phoned to say that he had had a massive heart attack and died. In fact, he had lived longer than expected and, faithful servant that he was, was serving his Lord in his church until the end.

Brenda is such a brave person! She had lived in the shadow of her husband's poor health for some years. She wanted John to go back to be with her and her (now adult) children, so he left immediately and stayed a little while, which I know was a real comfort for her. Some dear friends of the family paid his airfare, for which we were very grateful.

The following year, after John and I returned to England for good, we went to stay with Brenda for a while as soon as we could. She and David had married the same year as we did and 2003 would see our ruby wedding anniversary. Brenda organised a little celebration for us in her home.

From then on, we went to visit her frequently. How we enjoyed those times together! We got to know her – and Andrew and Stella – on a much deeper level and we became the very best of friends. I have turned to Brenda in my suffering of recent years and I thank the Lord for her love and kindness.

Andrew and Stella have comforted me, too. I love their enthusiasm for God and his Kingdom. Both John and I found them stimulating and challenging, and I still do.

Chapter 24

I want to tell some stories that stand out from those years in Orphaids.

A young woman I shall call 'Clara', who was in her late twenties, was very sick with systemic TB and was beyond any medical help. She had two small boys who were healthy – Daniel, aged seven, and Carlos, four – and a baby girl who died of Aids soon afterwards.

Matthew and Tricia looked after the baby, and all four of us were involved in caring for Clara, as well as giving her boys lots of tender loving care. In time, we were able to get some help – albeit slowly. We had wanted to involve Christian women from the local churches in this work, but sadly, as a result of ignorance and rather legalistic teaching, this proved difficult.

Naturally, Clara opened up and shared her life story with us. She had been a sex worker, but not from choice – her family had started her in this work. This was common practice in the port city of Guayaquil, where she had lived.

She was overwhelmed by the love and care we gave her and it was not long before she came to the Saviour. Her testimony was so beautiful, she would often have all of us who worked in Orphaids in tears. She would say, over and over again: 'I'm clean! I've been accepted by Jesus! I am loved!'

Her little boys were amazed by the transformation in her. We told them that one day, very soon, their mummy would go to be with Jesus, but they would have Jesus with them, 'right here'. 'He will take care of you,' we promised, 'and so shall we.'

The doctors had said she would last only a few weeks, but Clara was with us for almost a year. She was baptised in her bed and lots of carers, Orphaids staff and locals came to celebrate with her. What a happy day that was for the boys, and for other children from Orphaids – and of course for all us workers, too!

Slowly we saw her decline into the final stage of the illness, and those of us who were trained nurses shared the work of looking after her. Matthew and I were on duty the night she left this world. She shared with us her distress at leaving her children and we listened and comforted her as best we could. She wept and so did we – I vividly remember us sitting with her under the mosquito net. We said Psalm 23 together, and a short time later she died.

The next morning, Matthew and I washed her, dressed her in a pretty nightdress and combed her beautiful hair – she looked so young and lovely! Then we sent for Daniel and Carlos to say their goodbyes, and John and Tricia, and we all wept together!

Daniel and Carlos were placed in a house with one other boy and slowly they became more settled as their lives became more normal – though we still gave them opportunities to chat about their mother and how they were feeling.

Daniel did very well at high school. He came to the Lord and today is married to a lovely Christian woman, who is a trained midwife. They have two beautiful children.

Carlos never responded to the Saviour. After leaving Orphaids, he quite soon got into drugs and a few years ago took an overdose and died. We who had known and loved him were so saddened, and most of all Daniel and his wife, who had tried so hard to help him. So far as he knew, he had been Daniel's only living relative.

A very young couple came to us from the local hospital. Alfonso had full-blown Aids and Andrea, his wife, was HIV-positive. They lived for a time in one of the cabins in CLE, but after a few months it was obvious that Alfonso was becoming very sick and so we moved them into a flat.

They were evidently not interested in finding peace

and comfort. They were both so angry, they didn't help each other and were always miserable. Alfonso was in so much pain and distress, we were at a loss to know how to help him. John decided to take him to the mission hospital in Quito to see what could be done, but all to no avail.

When he came back, Alfonso became very introverted. We tried everything we could think of to give him relief and comfort, but he died in anguish of body and mind. I have nursed many dying people, but his death was the worst.

After that, Andrea decided to leave us. We heard only six months later that she, too, had died. What a sad end to two young lives!

There was a woman from the sierra named Rosa, who had four children: Ana, 12, Jon, 10, Richard, eight, and Edison, five. She had got the infection from her husband, who was already dead. The five of them had been abused dreadfully by his father, who would get into a terrible rage every day for some trivial reason and would beat them, Rosa included! All the children were traumatised, though their physical health was not too bad.

It was Matthew who went to fetch them, which was no small feat. It was a very long drive to the hovel where they lived, quite high up in the mountains, and there he was confronted by this belligerent old man.

A couple of hours into the journey down to New Horizons, he stopped to take them to a nice restaurant for a meal. He wanted also to give them some time to ask questions and relax a little, as they still had another four hours' drive ahead of them.

How sad and dispirited the five of them seemed when they arrived at Orphaids! Rosa was very sick, and certainly in no state to care for her children, so they were placed with an Orphaids family right away. They were able to tell their story, receive emotional and spiritual support and slowly settle in. Naturally, they could see their mother every day.

Rosa was most unusual for an Ecuadorian woman: she was slow to talk to anyone and, when she did, it was in such a quiet voice I had to strain to hear her. For some reason, she always wanted me, or, if I was not available, Matthew or John. I think it may have been that she thought she could trust us because we were foreigners.

All of us would talk to her about the Lord, but generally her response was to change the subject. We soon realised that what we had to do was to give her lots of loving care and really listen to her when she had something to say. Slowly, she began to open up with John and me, sobbing brokenly and trembling as she told us of all that had happened to her, and her dreadful fears for her children, and especially Ana.

All that John and I could do was to hold her close and tell her that God loved her, and that we loved her, too.

Edison's birthday was coming up, so we planned a party in our house to which all the children of Orphaids were invited. We made Rosa comfy in a recliner and what a lovely time we all had, with lots of the games and goodies little children love! Edison was so excited, and Rosa was smiling at last.

Two days later, one of the pastors from town came to see us in the evening. He told us that he felt the Lord had instructed him to visit all the people with Aids in Orphaids. John knew him well and gave him permission to do so. When he went out, John said: 'I think this could be a turning point in the attitude of many local Christians. It could make a big difference to those suffering with Aids in this area.'

The wonderful outcome of that evening was that that pastor led Rosa to the Saviour. She opened her heart and told him she had been overwhelmed by the love she had received. 'Why would these people even care?', she asked him.

His answer was that we loved Jesus, and that it was really Jesus who was showing his love to her through us. 'Then I need to know him,' she said. 'How do I do that?' So, our dear friend led her to him. She seemed to be burdened by a sense of guilt, he told us afterwards, so he encouraged her simply to tell the Lord she was sorry for whatever was on her conscience. A remarkable peace came over her then – it was as if she had let go of a heavy weight – and she became a different woman.

Rosa died just under a week later, and as she was dying she was actually praying for her children.

They all remained in Orphaids until they turned 16, except for Edison, who stayed until he was 18 so that he could finish high school. Today, the three older children are married. Jon and Richard are good, honest, hard-working citizens with children of their own. Ana, sadly, has not been able to have any. She is a Christian, but I'm not sure about the two older brothers.

Edison is now 23, a lovely Christian who, at the time of writing, is studying to be an electrical engineer. He keeps in touch with me – to him John and I are 'Grandpa' and 'Grandma'. He is a man his dear mother would be proud of.

Some of the children who came to us had very difficult physical issues. I have chosen to write about a girl I shall call 'Ester', who was so needy and at the same time so lovable.

She arrived with her mother, Ana, who was HIV-positive and had a six-month-old baby boy named Guido, who had been infected with Aids from birth. Ester was six and had a younger brother called Anderson. We put them in one of the flats, as Ana was not unwell at all and was quite capable of taking care of her family.

As soon as I saw Ester, my heart was deeply touched. The left side of her dear little face, her neck, her upper chest and the upper part of her left arm had been horribly scarred by burning kerosene. The scarring on her neck was pulling her face forwards and downwards, which had caused her bottom lip to ulcerate and made it hard for her to talk or eat.

I wanted immediately to take her into my arms, but I didn't, of course – I knew that she would need time to get used to me. John and I decided that we would let the family settle and get to know everyone in Orphaids while we considered what could be done for them. The baby was doing well on antiretroviral drugs obtained from the local hospital, but Ester's situation was more complex.

I discovered that her seventh birthday was coming up, so we threw a party for her in our house. What a lovely time she had that day! A few weeks later, I took her to the mission hospital in Quito to find out what could be done for her. She was seen by a consultant in burns of all kinds, who told me that she would need very complicated – and very expensive – plastic surgery to her face and neck.

When we got back to New Horizons, everyone on the Orphaids team was agreed that we should make this need known to our supporters both in Ecuador and in England. We believed that the Lord would provide, and our faith proved to be justified. Some money came in from England and a lot more from Ecuador – and a plastic surgeon at the mission hospital offered to do the operation free of charge, which greatly reduced the cost.

The date was set. John drove Ester and me up to Quito and the three of us booked into a missionary guesthouse near the hospital. Ester was admitted the next day. She was naturally afraid and tearful, but she calmed down when John assured her that I would stay with her and would be with her all the time. He himself had to go back to Orphaids, but I promised to keep in constant contact with him and her mother every day.

When the big day arrived, Ester and I prayed together. 'Lord Jesus,' she said, 'please help me to be brave, and look like everyone else.' I thanked the Lord for making this operation happen and asked him to help Ester throughout her stay in hospital.

Off she went then with a tearful little smile. Oh, how I desired and prayed with a full heart that all would be well!

When all was over and Ester was back in bed, several hours later, I sat at her bedside waiting for her to wake up. When she did, she whimpered a little, so I put my hand on her good arm and whispered: 'I'm still here. You're not alone.' She drifted back to sleep.

About two hours later, she resurfaced. The more awake she became, the more pain she felt, so a nurse came and gave her something to relieve it. That night, I was able to go back to the guesthouse for a couple of hours' sleep – but I was back at the hospital by 6am.

I found Ester sitting up, her face and neck covered in dressings. She looked a poor little thing, but her eyes brightened when she saw me. She couldn't talk, so she lifted her hand and waved.

Most of the pain she felt was where they had taken the skin graft, near the top of her leg. Moving was very difficult for her – she really cried every time she had to shift her position – but the nurses were very kind and very patient with her. With lots of love and painkillers, she began to improve. In fact, it was amazing how quickly she was healing!

After five days or so, the dressings were removed from Ester's face, though not her neck. The nurse gave her a mirror so that she could see herself. When she saw her reflection, red and raw, her eyes widened in fear; but the nurse assured her that the inflammation would slowly subside and then she would be really pretty!

I was delighted at the outcome. Her mouth was now normal and in very little time her face began to clear. She still had some scarring but it was nothing like it had been.

Ester had to stay in hospital for another week, so I decided to go into town and get her a present. I hoped I would see something that would distract her and cheer her up, and to my delight I found a darling dolly, about eight inches in length, with dark wavy hair to comb and a nice dress and shoes which she could take off.

When I got back to the hospital, Ester had just been walking and was distressed by the pain in her leg. After a little cuddle, I put her on the bed and said: 'I have something for a brave little girl called Ester.'

How thrilled she was, her eyes bright with expectation! When she saw the dolly, her delight was lovely to see. I can't remember the name she gave it, but it brought her such joy! When one of the nurses came in, she told her, as best she could: 'My grandma... this... for me.'

A few days later, we were told that she could go home once the surgeon had seen her the next day. He was very pleased with her progress, and she was discharged.

We stayed that night at the guesthouse and I arranged for John or Lenin, Orphaids' administrator, to come and get us the following afternoon. As a treat, I took Ester to the cinema in the morning, to see the very funny animated film *Ice Age*. She had never been to the cinema before and to hear this dear little girl laugh made my heart sing.

Ester is now in her late twenties. She lives in Quito and works as a community care nurse – she told me recently that she has worked non-stop for months because of Covid-19. I am still very much her grandma and she is constantly in touch with me, which brings me great joy. In my eyes, she is really beautiful, and to my delight she is also a faithful Christian.

Her mother, Ana, is still alive and well, and Guido, too – they live together near the coast. The last I heard of Anderson was that he was working in an evangelical church in Colombia and, among other things, playing in the music group.

Chapter 25

Not all of our residents in Orphaids were victims of Aids. One day, the child welfare people brought a little girl to us, four or five years of age. A young woman we knew named Rosalba, a committed Christian from one of the local churches, had seen her in a neighbour's yard, tethered to a tree with a cord tied round her ankle.

She had gone back later in the day and found the poor little thing still there. Indignantly, she had asked the woman: 'Why have you done this?'

The woman explained that the child's mother was a Colombian who had been in Ecuador illegally and had gone back to her country to get some papers. She had left the little one with her neighbours to look after until she came back, but she had been gone for some months now and the child was very difficult. They thought she must be 'retarded': she wouldn't obey them, she wouldn't eat anything and she was very smelly.

Why hadn't they called welfare, Rosalba asked. The woman said she didn't want to get involved, either with the authorities or with the child. Besides, she was afraid that the mother would be very angry with her if she did that.

Rosalba asked her: 'Do you know me, and where I live?' The woman said she did. Rosalba said: 'Let me take her, and if her mother comes back you'll know where to find her.' The little girl's name, she learnt, was (let's say) Johana.

After a few days, Rosalba realised that she had an infection in both ears and was in considerable pain, so she decided to call welfare after all. They were at a loss to know either where they could place the child safely or where they could get her treated. At this point, Rosalba told them about Orphaids, and so she came to us.

We welcomed her, and then gave her a thorough

examination. It turned out that she had been born with a cleft palate and that was why she couldn't talk, and how her ears had become infected. She was evidently also deeply disturbed by the neglect and cruelty she had suffered.

At that time, we had a missionary couple with us from the north of England, Simeon and Catherine, who were acting as houseparents. Besides their own small daughter they were already looking after two little girls. We all felt that they would be the best people to care for a child with so many needs.

At first, little Johana wouldn't even get into bed and instead slept on the floor, and she would eat only rice with tomato sauce. It took months of hard work to bring about even the smallest changes in her behaviour – but the patience and love that Simeon and Catherine showed her were wonderful and slowly she began to trust people.

Soon, plans were being made to repair her palate.

Several months after Johana joined us, my daughter Ana brought a team of psychotherapists from England to Orphaids to do some work with the staff on the grief and trauma that most of our children had experienced and how we should treat them.

We all benefited so much from this instruction. One of Ana's party was a member of the House of Lords, Lord Stone, who was interested in her work and had come as an observer. He was really helped himself by what the team taught us and he was enthusiastic about all we were doing in Orphaids.

As a thankyou, we decided that we should treat the team to an Ecuadorian cultural experience. We took them to the Mitad del Mundo ('Centre of the World') in the foothills of the Andes close to Quito. Ecuador is on the Equator and here tourists can pose for photographs with one foot in each hemisphere. Indigenous people in tribal dress congregate there, selling handicrafts, and there is the dearest little church standing right on the line.

Simeon and Catherine had never been there, so they and the children in their household were included in our party. When we arrived, some men were playing beautiful Andean music, and to our amazement Johana went up close to them and, overjoyed, began dancing around to the rhythm. Lord Stone was so moved by this that he went over and danced with her, while the rest of us clapped in time.

While I was in the mission hospital with Ester, Johana was admitted to have her palate repaired. Simeon and Catherine were with her until the operation was over and I was able to look out for her after they had to return to New Horizons.

After Ana had spent some time with Johana, she told us that, far from being mentally disabled, she thought she might actually be of above-average intelligence. This turned out to be the case – she excelled in school, right from first grade until she finally left us a little before she turned 18.

Johana is now married, with a young son. She often sends me photos of herself and her family.

Finally, I must tell the story of a young Christian from the high Andes who I shall call 'Juan Carlos'. As I write this, just the thought of that dear fellow brings tears to my eyes. He was so Christlike; there was this peace about him. Even in his most awful times of suffering, you felt he knew that Jesus was standing near him.

He was someone I have felt honoured to have known. He had a profound impact on my life.

Juan Carlos had cystic fibrosis, which was now at an advanced stage, and living at high altitude with his condition was putting his life in danger. A local doctor who had been treating him ever since he was small had heard about Orphaids, so he came to see us on the off-chance we could help Juan Carlos by housing and caring for him. His village was 10,000 feet above sea level, while CLE was only 2,000 feet.

We happened to have a flat empty at the time and so it was arranged that he should come. His parents had a small truck and a week later they brought not only Juan Carlos but beds for him and themselves, as they hoped they could stay some weekends to help with his care. He was 18 years old when he came to us, and looked so frail!

The change of location made a big difference and in a week or two he was able to stand and walk. To give him something to do, John set up a little shop in his flat where he could sell dry foods and tinned foods, tea and coffee, a few cleaning materials and some sweets the children of Orphaids could buy with any pocket money they had. In this way, Juan Carlos was able to earn a little to get things for himself.

Later, when he was even stronger, he would help the builders on the site by carrying messages and occasionally getting them a cold drink.

He was a very quiet person, gentle in all his ways and very grateful for any help. He loved to talk to John mostly, usually about his faith and his relationship with Jesus or about his family. He did converse with the rest of us, but it was John he really loved to be with. John, too, was a quiet man of gentle ways and they were comfortable in each other's company.

The serenity Juan Carlos had about him made him very calming. We all loved him – he touched everyone he met. The workmen, most of whom were not Christians, thought he was really an angel in disguise!

He lived in Orphaids for three years. His death was like something out of the scriptures.

It was a day like any other day there – quite busy, as ever, but more than usually so for me as John had gone to Quito to see the lawyer. He had left a message for me to be sure to visit Juan Carlos as he had not been feeling well the previous night.

It would have been about mid morning that I looked in on him and found him struggling to breathe. I called for help and we sat him up and gave him oxygen. He could hardly speak, but he made it clear that he was in deep trouble. Someone had to stay with him all the time.

I found out that his father had been in touch to say he would be in the area on business and was going to be calling late that afternoon. The woman who was helping me with Juan Carlos was breaking down emotionally; I needed her to concentrate, so I said to her: 'Sonya, we have to be brave and trust the Lord. Will you pray for all of us, and especially Juan Carlos, and the Lord will see us through.'

About 4pm, Juan Carlos began to fail. His colour was awful. I started to pray quietly very near to his ear and he managed to ask me where his father was. I assured him he was coming soon. When he arrived, Juan Carlos whispered to him that what he wanted more than anything was that one of his brothers should surrender to Jesus. 'Tell him this is my prayer,' he said.

His father prayed and then Juan Carlos said, quite audibly: 'I am finished.' He rested his head on his father's arm and breathed his last. It was as if he had waited until he could give him that message.

Needless to say, we were all weeping quietly, but once he had died, his father, Sonya and I held each other and sobbed!

I confess that I cried because that lovely, dear boy was now at peace. Also, because I was so moved by his selflessness right to the very end! Juan Carlos was 21 when he went to be with his Lord. In his short but very meaningful life, he had radiated God's glory.

John was greeted with the news of Juan Carlos's passing when he got back from Quito. He was deeply saddened and went immediately to see his father, who was quite broken, if also relieved for his son.

It was not possible to get Juan Carlos certified as dead in Santo Dom because legally his body would have to be disposed of within 24 hours and the people of his village, far off in the Andes, would want him to be buried there. So, after much deliberation, his father decided that he should take him home that night and get him certified dead there, by the doctor who had cared for him over many years.

John was worried about police checkpoints, but Juan Carlos's father was adamant. In the end, John was persuaded to accompany him, holding the body in the back seat as if it was merely asleep. It was going to be a long trip! Before they set off, John treated the body with formaldehyde to slow decomposition until they got to the cooler air of the mountains. We all prayed together and off they went.

I had a hard time sleeping that night. What a day it had been!

I received a phone call early the next morning. They had reached the village without any problems; the funeral was to be that afternoon and John had been asked to give 'a word from the Lord'.

Late that afternoon, I got another call from John. He told me that it was the most amazing funeral he had ever witnessed – there were hundreds of people there from quite far afield. He couldn't think how they had all learnt of Juan Carlos's death so quickly! (He was still puzzled by this many years later.)

When he finally got home by bus the following day, he was exhausted.

About five months after Juan Carlos went to glory, we had a surprise visit from his parents. They wanted to see us again to thank us for all we had done for their son and to tell us that, a week or so earlier, the brother he had prayed for had come to know the Lord. How thrilled we were to hear such wonderful news!

Also, they said that Juan Carlos had secretly saved some money so that they could get us a present from him. He knew exactly what we would like: I had mentioned to him some ceramic bells I had seen in Otavalo which tinkled prettily when the breeze caught them. Apparently, I had drawn John over to see them. I don't know why we didn't buy them, as he, too, thought them very beautiful.

I have a vague recollection of that conversation with Juan Carlos. Maybe I was just passing the time of day with him. I knew he had been to Otavalo and liked the huge craft market there.

His parents had gone to Otavalo and found the bells and bought them, and here they were giving them to us in Juan Carlos's name. Naturally, we were thrilled with them, and deeply moved that he had thought to do such a thing. It was so typical of him!

Today, those bells have pride of place in our sitting room in New Horizons, where they hang from the high ceiling. It is a long time since I have been there, but whenever I used to hear their tinkling I would catch Juan Carlos's dear, soft, gentle voice – *Buenos días, Brendita* or *Dios le bendiga, Brendita* – and I would thank the Lord for having met a man like him.

Chapter 26

In 2003, John and I semi-retired, as his health was now causing concern. He had suffered a minor heart attack in 1997 while playing tennis when we were home on furlough. I had had to return to Ecuador on my own to sort out some problems in Orphaids, while John had stents fitted in his main coronary artery.

As soon as he got back to New Horizons, two months later, he resumed working at his usual pace. After a year or so, I could see that he was really feeling the strain and I pleaded with him to slow down – at least to reduce the amount of preaching he took on. Much to my amazement, he did.

He began to feel unwell in 2001, being exhausted and unable to cope. I felt strongly that he needed to let some of his responsibilities go and we had many conversations about this. His workload as team leader of Latin Link Ecuador (which involved supporting all their missionaries there) and as acting director of Orphaids, as well as the work of preaching and teaching with the churches in Santo Dom, was taking its toll on him physically – and, I had noticed, mentally, too: he was forgetting things and getting things mixed up.

I was anxious that we should go back to England to have him checked, and when he had another minor heart attack in early 2001, it accelerated all our plans. A doctor flew out to accompany John back to England and take him by car to our daughter Mary's house. She then took him to see his cardiologist.

I so wanted to be with him, but John had begged me to stay in New Horizons to take care of things in Orphaids. We prayed about it a lot and began to think that we might be coming to the end of our time in Ecuador. Finally, we came to the decision that I would stay there until he returned and then, without any more delay, we would plan what we were going to do thereafter.

He joined me a few months later, after he had had some more stents put in, but only to sort things out finally and for us both to say '*Hasta la vista!*' to all our friends and colleagues.

Having promised faithfully that we would visit them again when we could, John and I landed back in England in August 2003. Initially, we were housesitting for various friends while they were on holiday, and then we rented Ana and Kevin's house in Hawkhurst, as they were living in Northwood at the time in accommodation that went with Kevin's job.

We wanted to celebrate our ruby wedding anniversary in November with all our family. Mary hosted the party at her house and not one member of the family was missing (except those yet to be born!).

Ana had organised a photographer and the pictures he took are a real joy. We had one of them enlarged and it hangs on the wall where I sit writing. It holds such precious memories!

The following February, John had to go back to Ecuador for a while. Before he went, he ordered a lovely little red rose bush from our local florist and entrusted to Mary a card to give me on Valentine's Day. He wrote in it:

> My darling Brenda, I will be missing you today and each day that I am away. Thank you for encouraging me to go to Ecuador yet again!
>
> I am taking with me especially the words [Mary's daughter] Alice gave to [her brother] John on his baptism... 'In all your ways acknowledge Him and He will make your paths straight.'
>
> I love you with all my heart. God bless you, my darling xx

Like all the lovely things John ever wrote to me, that card

is a treasure to me. He, too, saved all my cards and letters to him.

Matthew and Tricia returned to England in 2005. At that point, they had four boys – a fifth was to arrive the following year. Tricia wanted to go back into nursing and, after doing a refresher course, got a part-time job, so in 2006 I started caring for her two littlest ones until she or Matthew got home.

I would catch a couple of buses to their house in Maidstone very early so that I could take Phillip to his primary school (and, after a year or so, Ben to nursery). During the day, I would sort out the evening meal for them all. Later, I would take Ben in the pushchair to collect Phillip from school. What fun they both were! Phillip would skip along beside me, chattering about all sorts of things. One day, he told me he had a girlfriend called Emily and he was going to marry her when he was all grown up.

The things that dear fellow said were quite hilarious. One day, he told me he now knew the difference between boys and girls. 'Wow!', I said. 'Tell me, I would love to know!' 'You're old,' said Phillip, 'you must know already.' 'Yes, but I want to know what *you* know.' He stopped and turned to face me. 'Well,' he said solemnly, 'you girls have to sit on the toilet. We boys don't.'

As you can imagine, I was very amused by this.

I used to take him through his reading books, and then we set the table together. Ben was usually asleep all the while, still in his pushchair.

The three bigger lads would come home not long after, and what fun and games we had until their mum or dad got in! The memory of those Hart boys as they were then will always fill me with happiness – and now as young men they bring me immense joy!

After that school year was over, John joined me in taking

care of the boys. This made things so much easier for me, as we drove there. Taking the bus could be miserable in winter, especially waiting for connections. I was glad when John decided that he would still go with me when the new school year started.

Mary and Alan needed help as well, as they were both having to set off for work quite early. John would go round to their house and do devotions with John and Alice, who would already be dressed and breakfasted by the time he arrived. They so loved their times with Grandpops, and he often remarked on the joy it gave him just to be with them.

We regularly travelled up to Northwood to see Ana, Kevin and Sky, and even more often after Ana gave birth to Luke. Out of deep love for Sky, who was a promising athlete, John took up running, too, and took part in one or two all-age five-kilometre 'parkruns'.

Our last few years in Hawkhurst and, from 2007, our first few in Eastbourne gave us wonderful times with all of our grandchildren. How we both loved them, and what a privilege it was to be involved in their lives! Today, Matthew's older sons show real concern for me; they often ring me, and it's always so stimulating to hear their news. John Digman phones me, too, and the others communicate often, usually by a message on Facebook.

For John and me, a new stage of life was in store. We remained committed to Orphaids, and John was to go back to New Horizons every year for five years or so; but otherwise we had no plans, or even any ideas, as to what lay ahead.

We knew we were still the Lord's servants and felt that we must be open to his will. For what purpose had he brought us back to England?

John had had to have more treatment for his heart problem, but in 2005 he was told that there was nothing more that could be done for him by surgical means. From now on, his condition was to be controlled by medication.

Another problem was now creeping up on us. I had begun to see changes in John's behaviour during the last year we spent in Ecuador. His memory was affected and as a result he would often get confused and make mistakes that seemed very out of character.

By 2005, it had become a real worry – I was having to watch out for him, still letting him do things but trying to ensure that he didn't get muddled and didn't suffer any unnecessary stress. However, I put it all down to John's cardiac problem and thought that with time and enough rest he would improve.

He continued to go to Ecuador, and sometimes I went with him. I couldn't always accompany him as we paid our own airfares, which rather stretched our resources. John seemed to manage well and his presence there was always hugely encouraging to the director, a Colombian psychologist called Luz Celly Piamba Paz, and her staff.

After four years living in the village of Hawkhurst, where John had been a Baptist minister from 1980 to 1993, we relocated to Eastbourne towards the end of 2007. The Childs Charitable Trust, which was chaired by our close friend Derek Martin, one of the deacons at Hawkhurst Baptist, had provided us with a lovely bungalow for a peppercorn rent.

We moved in late December and, while John returned to Ecuador in January for a month, I started looking for a church. I went to a couple within walking distance of our new home but didn't find one that, on reflection, seemed suitable for us.

We had heard about Victoria Baptist Church and, when John got back, we went to try it out. By the end of a fantastic service, with great Bible teaching, we both felt we had come home! And that's how it was to feel for all the nine years we went there.

Within a few months, John was asked to preach. We joined the world mission prayer group and a house group – we were so blessed! We loved that house group, which was led by a sheep farmer named Richard and Margaret, his wife. Richard and Margaret are the kindest and most caring of people and they were to prove an immense support to us both – and me especially.

The following year, John accepted an invitation to chair the church's 'world mission council'. He loved that job – he always had vision! He introduced the church to organisations involved in very different types of mission work. For example, he got an MAF team to come for a weekend and they brought with them a single-engine plane for people to look at. What a stimulus that was to all!

He and I also did a stint as street pastors, for a little over two years. I had to stop during our second winter, owing to a prolonged chest infection; but John carried on without me for another six months.

A few weeks into 2009, it was becoming obvious that he was doing too much. I begged him to cut back on his activities in the church, and by the end of that year he did so. He also reduced his trips to Ecuador.

We did go back together in 2012, and I could see then – possibly for the first time – that something very serious was happening. Getting through immigration when we were changing flights in America was a nightmare: John would not let me take care of the paperwork and he got into a real panic. It was awful to see his distress, he was trembling so badly.

We were met at the airport in Quito by a longstanding friend, Sheila Leech. She worked for the mission hospital and led medical emergency-response teams that flew to any type of disaster anywhere in the world. We first met her when she was doing missionary work in the area around Santo Dom.

We were to spend a while with Sheila to get over our long flight. It was such fun to be with her again! We both loved her company – she is a great comic and mimic and can tell the most hilarious stories, doing all the characters with different accents! She has always encouraged us and been a very good friend to us.

After we had been with her for a day, she called me into the garden and, with tears in her eyes, asked me: 'What's happening to our lovely John?' She said she thought he had suffered a severe loss of short-term memory – which only confirmed my suspicions.

I told her that I had begged him to go to the doctor but he didn't see that he had a problem at all.

Sheila managed to get John to see a neurologist. He was the son of Dr Bosano, a lovely Christian lawyer who had been a very good friend of ours when we first went to Ecuador. Dr Bosano was a leading figure at the Central University of Ecuador and an amazingly influential man. One dreadful day, he was kidnapped – and he was never found. His sons had been devastated, and John had helped them through their ordeal.

John remembered William Bosano and a consultation was soon arranged. After the scans and the other clinical assessments had been done, William told us that John did indeed have a serious problem. He gave him some medication, but not a diagnosis.

A month or so later, it was amazing what a difference the medication had made. We were rather relieved and very thankful.

As soon as we got back to England, we went to see our GP. He told us that we would have to take John's results to a place in Eastbourne that specialised in mental-health problems. My heart sank, though I still didn't voice my fears.

We duly went, and handed over all the material we had brought back with us from Ecuador. After a long wait, a psychiatrist called us into his consulting room, sat us down and informed us that John had vascular dementia. What a shock that was for him! He was shattered.

The psychiatrist went on to explain that John 'would have to stay on the medication now', though normally it would not have been prescribed on the NHS as it is very expensive. William Bosano had done John a great favour, he said, as it would keep him stable for a few years yet. And so it did.

In 2013, we celebrated our golden wedding anniversary with a service in our church, of thanksgiving and praise for all we owed to our wonderful God, without whose love and protection we would surely have floundered. How gracious our Lord is, that he takes the weak and failing and uses them for his glory! For the reading, we chose Psalm 98: 'Sing to the LORD a new song, for he has done marvellous things.'

As a surprise, there was a live link from Ecuador: Luz Celly greeted us and some of the children there sang to us. Our whole family took part in the service – our nine grandchildren sang together 'How great is our God'. Ben, at the age of seven, had written his own prayer for us and he said it after they had finished singing.

Afterwards, we all had an 'English tea' – dainty sandwiches and a variety of cakes, served with tea and coffee – presented by the church's catering group. John and I cut a lovely anniversary cake, baked and decorated by Ellen Hannavy-Cousen, a dear friend since Hawkhurst days. It really was an amazing occasion! Ana had asked someone to take photographs – I have one of John and me on display in my sitting room. I also love the one of the whole family which is in the beautiful album she put together for us.

At this stage, John was still able to write, his handwriting always neat and clear. He wrote this in his card to me, adapting the words from Proverbs 31:

My dearest wife of 50 years
YOU are...
A wife of noble character...
I have full confidence in you...
You bring me good, not harm...
You open your arms to the poor
And extend your hands to the needy...
You are clothed with strength and dignity...
You speak with wisdom...
Your children call you blessed and I praise
    you:
'Many women do noble things,
But you surpass them all.'
So...
I thank YOU VERY much for these, so very
    wonderful years.
My admiration and love keeps on growing.
I give you ALL my love and respect.
I am always your John x

In 2014, our eldest grandson, John, who at the time was
leading the Christian Union at Reading University, asked
his grandpops to speak at an event they were putting on.
My husband was still fairly fluent in his speech at this
juncture, and still able to write; but at first he said no, in
case he might let them down. Our grandson persisted,
and eventually John said yes.

He spoke on the sovereignty of God. Before he began,
he told his audience that he had been diagnosed with
vascular dementia and asked them to bear with him if
he should lose his thread.

His talk was amazing. Its content was inspired, and in
delivering it he never stumbled once. When he finished,
he got a standing ovation – it really was quite emotional.
Afterwards, so many of the students wanted to speak with
him. The whole experience was very encouraging for him.

Chapter 27

It was not until the following year that we began to see further deterioration in John. He began to lose his speech then and he went through a really dark time emotionally. Some things that happened were very distressing.

On one occasion, we went into town just before Christmas to do some shopping for the little members of the family and we visited a lovely toyshop in the shopping mall. After five minutes, John became very restless and told me: 'That's enough. I want some books' (W H Smith was just round the corner).

'Let me finish here,' I said, 'and then I'll go with you.' Quite crossly, he said: 'No, I can go on my own. I'll come back here for you.' And off he went. I was very concerned that he might forget where I was, so after getting a couple of things I made my way to Smith's. He wasn't there.

I hurried back to the toyshop, but he was not there, either. What a sense of panic I felt! I must have spent 15 minutes debating what to do. I asked someone where the police station was and was just on my way when John came into view. I could have wept with relief! He had gone to C & H Fabrics to find me (I was forever knitting for the family, so we went there quite often and always had tea and cake there).

'Why didn't you come?', he demanded. 'I've been waiting there for ages.' With an exasperated sigh, he explained that I '*always* go to C & H Fabrics'. The staff had given him a cup of tea and, after a while, had asked him where I was. 'I said you were buying Christmas presents for our grandchildren, so they sent me here.'

What a lesson that was for me, never to lose sight of him when we were out!

Once we were walking to our local shops and had got halfway when he decided he wanted to go home. Rather than argue with him, I said: 'OK, we'll go back.' 'No, no, no,' said John, quite forcefully. 'I can go back on my own. You go on!'

So, I acted as if I was going on, but after a little while I looked back – just in time to see him take the wrong turning. I walked back quickly and found him looking very lost and awfully upset. I took his arm and gently guided him in the right direction.

For quite some time, John had been very anxious about Orphaids and he kept talking about going back to New Horizons to see everyone there, especially the children. I had a word with his doctor and he said: 'It could be risky, but if you and your family are wanting to make him happy, then go ahead!' And so in 2016 we did.

Mary was much in favour of us going, and she and my niece Ali came too to take care of us. Alan came out later, as Ali had to go back, so that John and I could stay for a month in total. It really did take two to look after him!

At first, things were very difficult. After we had been there two days, I thought: What have I done? John didn't know where he was. He would fade in and out of clarity, and would wander into other people's rooms and take things. Often, he would pretend that he recognised people but would ask me afterwards: 'Who are they?'

After another day or so, however, he was out with the Orphaids children most days. They would come to the house and ask for '*Abuelito*' and he would be off like a shot to have fun with them! He had always loved children but in his dementia he was absolutely fascinated by them.

John wanted to say his goodbyes to everyone, so a service was held in El Buen Pastor, the mother church he and I had helped to found in 1970, with invitations sent to all the other churches in and around Santo Dom. Many people came and it was a wonderful occasion.

A similar meeting took place at Orphaids, which some of our dear Christian Colorados came to. How thrilled John was to see them! They, too, were so pleased to have a chance to say their farewells and give him a hug.

Once we were back in England, John was so much more at peace about the Lord's work in Ecuador. It was as if he had closed a door. He loved looking at photos of the work and the children, but he very rarely mentioned them thereafter.

That same year, our second-eldest grandson, James, was to marry Beth, his lovely sweetheart from his teenage years. He asked his grandpops if he would do the prayers after they had made their vows. John asked one of the nurses who visited us for help. He was afraid he might lose his place, so she printed out the prayers for him in very large letters, with every topic in a different colour.

When the day of the wedding arrived, John said that he would be fine and wouldn't need me to go up with him. However, when it came to it he took hold of my hand and, once we got to the front, wanted me to read the prayers. I gave them back to him and signalled to him to go ahead – which he did, in a tremulous voice.

His children and grandchildren, and especially James and Beth, saw the great effort he was making and his evident sincerity and wept.

Both of us had done a lot of weeping and consoling each other in the early months. Later on, when the condition was more advanced, it was a dreadful time for us, and especially John. For a while, he felt abandoned by God. Nonetheless, the Lord comforted, guided and blessed us. I certainly sensed his dear presence.

I must tell you of one lovely thing that happened, in 2018. It was night-time in winter. John was up a lot in the night and generally I would hear him and go and bring him back to bed. On this occasion I must have been deeply asleep, because when I did get up to find him out of bed he had evidently been up for quite some time, as he was very cold and unhappy.

I fetched his nice, cosy dressing gown and put it on him, but before I tied the belt around him I pulled him close to give him a hug and warm him up. John took the two ends of the belt and tied them around us both, saying, as best he could, 'I love you, I love you,' over and over again. When I looked into his face, he was smiling but there were tears in his eyes.

John always managed to convey his love and appreciation for me. As his speech became less clear, he wrote cards to me instead. Some days, he would spend hours on a card. His handwriting became like that of a seven-year-old, and eventually he couldn't even sign his name.

I want to share some of the cards he gave me over the years. One, from 2009, is so special to me that I have always kept it in my bedroom:

> My darling Brenda...
> Today is our 46th anniversary of our marriage. To me it is very special.
> Two thirds of my life we have been husband and wife.
> Thank you for every one of the 16,801 days we have been married.
> Thank you for always loving me, even when I was less than lovable.
> Thank you for being my wife, lover, partner and the mother of our children.
> Also, thank you too for being my partner in all that God has called us to do.
> I thought I loved you in 1963, and I did, but now I love you really, because I truly know you, and you know me, and I know you truly love me.
> Let's enjoy today.
> With ALL my love
> John xxx

For that anniversary, he had booked a table at the Grand Hotel in Eastbourne as a surprise for me. It was such a special time with my lovely John.

Another card, when he could hardly write at all, was for Christmas:

> A happy Christmas for the one I love...
> And!
> Thank you for being the most precious loved one...
> All through the years you have been the one who has enabled me to flourish and together God has blessed us in his service for many wonderful years. xx

Here is a portion of a birthday card that took him a whole day to write:

> Thank you darling for being with me all these years, I have never ever regretted making those vows in 1963 that made us one.
> Wherever we have gone, whatever we have done, I have always known that we are ONE, our respective strengths have enabled us to serve our God and so many people, we could not have done this without our great God and our oneness, also our strong faith, and our deep love for each other!
> With ALL my love.
> John x

A time came in 2017 when John no longer liked going to church. He was becoming more introverted, and being with a lot of people, even people he had known for many years, exhausted and distressed him. When I could no longer leave him alone to go myself, I started to put him in a day centre on Sunday mornings. How he hated that!

I would find him so very unhappy when I went to collect him. It saddened me immensely, so after a couple of months I stopped going to church myself. We decided then that we could 'do church' at home. Every morning and evening, we would pray for a while, read the Bible and then listen to some familiar Christian music, which was a real comfort to John.

He loved the evenings especially. Once he was in bed, I would sing from an old book hymns he had known as a child and others we had sung together in our younger days. Often I would sing to him our wedding hymn 'O the deep, deep love of Jesus!'. He would lie there contentedly, holding my hand and smiling.

I also read the scriptures to him whenever I saw him in distress. I had come to understand that mental suffering can be worse than physical pain.

The slow stripping away of John's ability to think and communicate caused me real anguish. We had been so close in heart and mind and spirit for most of our lives together that the growing distance between us brought back traumatic memories of our early married life.

This experience was a deep refining of my soul. I became more aware that, in a sense, the Lord had always been my spouse, as the lover of my soul. Now, he really did become my husband. The love and tenderness he bathed me in through the darkest times were oh, so very comforting and strengthening!

When I knelt at my bedside to weep and pray, I often felt that the Saviour was kneeling and weeping with me, and interceding on my behalf.

I realised early in 2018 that I needed to be nearer my children. John was more confused at night and couldn't rest, and so I couldn't rest, either. I had lost weight, and that had made me weaker. A recent scan of my liver that showed that it was enlarged, had alarmed my doctor – and me!

So, in May we moved back to Hawkhurst, to live in a very nice alms flat with a bedroom, a sitting room, a kitchen and a shower room. It is set in lovely grounds, in a complex run by a trust (and very well run, too).

Naturally, the move was traumatic for John. The flat is small but he would still get lost looking for whichever room it was he wanted.

Mary arranged for a young woman to come to shower him twice a week (she would leave the room sparkling clean every time, and even did some hoovering for me as well!). Sharon is so lovely – John got used to her and she gradually became a friend to me. She regularly came to church with me, and remains in my prayers.

Later that year, it became impossible for one person to manage John at night, so one or other of our children would come and help. This was not sustainable, though, because all three of them have very demanding jobs and are also very active in their local churches.

For Christmas, the social services got him placed in respite care so that I could have a complete break.

In the new year, he had a nasty fall in the entrance hall to the flat and had to go into care again.

Meanwhile, I had had three biopsies of my liver done and the outcome was that I had only a small amount of functioning liver left. The consultant said it was impossible for me to have treatment while I was caring for John.

Our children organised a family get-together at which they made it clear to me that they were convinced it was now time for their dad to go into permanent care. It took an awful struggle for me to come to the point where I committed the most precious person in my life to the hands of others; but physically I was becoming weaker by the day and less able to manage, so I knew that this was the right thing to do.

After a fair bit of haggling, Mary managed to persuade social services that John should go into a Christian care home in Tunbridge Wells. This place was amazing. The love and tenderness that all the staff expressed in the physical care they gave him spoke of the presence of the Saviour in their lives.

John settled in well, and most of the time he was at peace. I would visit him three times a week. Matthew's son Peter, who had just finished a thesis in neuroscience, told me that emotional memory lasts much longer than cognitive memory and so the fact I had shown Grandpops affection and told him how much I loved him would have left him with a warm feeling even though he wouldn't remember me being there.

As time went by, John became less and less mobile. At first, I was able, with Anna Lisa, to take him into the sitting room, where there was a two-seater settee, which meant that I could be close to him physically, hugging him and showing him lots of affection.

Later, we had to leave it to the staff to get him up out of his chair and standing, and so it became more difficult to move him.

I was now being treated myself, and I was enjoying my new freedom – not least, worshipping once more in the Baptist church in the village that holds so many wonderful memories. This was such a lovely gift from my Lord to me! There are still a few people who were there when John was the minister; they are quite elderly now, but they still recall that wonderful time in the life of the church – and the story of our family.

However, I was put on a high dose of steroids for four months, which unfortunately had some very adverse side-effects. I was also, after a while, struggling emotionally. I missed John's companionship and experienced an acute sense of loss that plunged me into bouts of weeping. I felt anguished and bewildered, crushed and oh, so alone – and ashamed of my inability to control my feelings!

In turmoil, I would tell the Lord all my conflicting

thoughts and ask him to help, and I began to hear him whispering: 'Brenda, I am all you need. I am the way forward. Focus on me! I am with you in all that is happening.'

Each day, as I contemplated the life of my Saviour and his love and mercy, these awful attacks diminished and I was once again able to thank and praise God for all his care for both John and me and all the grace he has lavished on us.

That respite didn't last. In March 2020, Britain went into lockdown because of the coronavirus that was spreading fast all over the world. I was contacted and told that I was considered extremely vulnerable and should be 'shielding' myself. The care home where John was was now closed to all visitors.

I became more and more depressed. John must be feeling that we don't care about him, I thought. He won't understand my absence. I was missing him acutely myself. It was as if he was already dead, and yet he was still there. Before, when I consoled him I had also found consolation myself; now, I was feeling his pain in being separated as well as my own.

Day and night, I was plagued by negative thoughts about my past and beset by memories of feeling so very alone. A great fog seemed to engulf me, until I was crying out in desperation, 'Lord, help me, PLEASE!' At one time, the mental pain was so awful that I felt I was having a breakdown.

I also felt very guilty about my attitude regarding wounds from years ago. However, I was able to tell the Lord about these feelings and that helped me.

I decided that I needed to soak my mind and soul in the word of God, so I committed myself to relearning texts I had known by heart for most of my life but which had begun to slip my memory.

The first was 2 Corinthians 10:5, and especially the

second half: 'We demolish arguments and every pretension that sets itself up against the knowledge of God, and we take captive every thought to make it obedient to Christ.' I wrote the whole verse out and stuck it up in my kitchen, my bedroom and my sitting room. What a help that was!

I revised a number of psalms I had memorised in the past – especially Psalms 34, 103 and 139 – and posted them all over the flat. Also, other scriptures, such as Isaiah 40:31:

> ... Those who hope in the LORD
> will renew their strength.
> They will soar on wings like eagles;
> they will run and not grow weary,
> they will walk and not be faint.

Still, it took time to regain any sense of normality. One day I would be doing well, but I would be sobbing again during the night.

And then, unexpectedly, on the 26th July, while dozing in his wheelchair after a good breakfast, John died. I was shocked rigid when Mary and Alan came to tell me. For days, I was numb – I could not believe it had happened. I had caught a glimpse of him through a glass door two weeks earlier, but I had not seen him properly since March.

It was a real battle for me to gain any control over my emotions. The sense of loss and the deep, dark sadness that permeated my being were overwhelming. I had no one to give me a hug or say a prayer with me. I can't really put into words how painful it was.

Thankfully, I began to hear the Saviour's gentle voice once more and slowly I focused my mind and heart on him. The words of some lovely Christian song would pop into my head and bless me immensely, and I was able to praise and thank him for his everlasting love.

After a month or so, I could feel relieved that John had

died the way he had. Knowing him, he had slipped away exactly as he would have wanted to, without any fuss. I felt glad for his sake that he was now at peace.

Epilogue

Today, in July 2021, I still miss my precious John. I am continually aware of the great joy we shared in the Lord, and I am so very thankful for the wonderful life we had together in Hawkhurst and latterly in Ecuador, and for our fantastic children and grandchildren.

What blessings John and I knew in God's service! How humbling it is that he could use people such as us, so weak and failing! What amazing grace he lavished on us and our family! I am conscious of it all the time. All the praise, all the glory are his. Hallelujah, what a Saviour!

The Lord brought John and me together for both his purposes and our own good. We grew together and enjoyed a deep oneness. We knew our heavenly Father's love in his protection of us, our marriage and our children.

There is a lot of talk in our society about love. It helps to know what love is – and is not. As 1 Corinthians 13:4–8a puts it: 'Love is patient, love is kind. It does not envy, it does not boast, it is not proud. It does not dishonour others, it is not self-seeking, it is not easily angered, it keeps no record of wrongs. Love does not delight in evil but rejoices with the truth. It always protects, always trusts, always hopes, always perseveres. Love never fails.'

My story has truly been a love story. God so loved me, he gave his only Son to redeem me. He called me, too, to take up my cross and follow him. To take up the cross, a symbol of suffering – this is the reality when we truly want to be involved in following the God-man, the Lord Jesus Christ, surrendering all to him and submitting to his will.

I have learnt to thank the Lord for his loving presence, his written word and all the support and direction I have received – even when the pain was so much that I wanted to die and go to be with him! My God has never failed me. He understands my distress and confusion and is always faithful.

My own health issues have not gone away. I will always now have to be on immunosuppressant medication – although if the next drug gives me the awful side-effects I have experienced in the past, I have decided that quality of life is more important than longevity.

In my recent afflictions, I have been able to thank God in a new way. The words of this lovely Christian song come to mind:

> In your grace, you know where I walk,
> You know when I fall, you know all my
>   ways.
> In your love, I know you allow
> What I cannot grasp
> To bring you praise.
>
> *Thank you for the trials,*
> *For the fire, for the pain.*
> *Thank you for the strength,*
> *Knowing you have ordained*
> *Every day.*
>
> Your great power is shown when I'm
>   weak.
> You help me to see your love in this
>   place.
> Perfect peace is filling my mind
> And drawing my heart
> To praise you again.
>
> *In my uncertainty, your word is all I*
>   *need*
> *To know you're with me every day.*

(I should say that the first two lines of the refrain trouble me. I do not believe that life's adversities come from God: we live in a fallen world and have fallen natures. All of us suffer disappointment, sorrow and grief to some degree – though some more than others!)

I want to end with some words of Eddie Askew from his book of meditations and prayers *Disguises of Love*, which was published by the Leprosy Mission in 1983:

Disguises of Love
1 John 4:9–12

'Love', says Han Suyin the author, 'is a many-splendoured thing.' So it is. Shimmering like crystal, its rainbow beams sparkling, picking up the smallest ray of light and turning life into a rich spectrum of colour. That's the easy bit. That's the sort of love I can accept. That's the love I can identify and rejoice in without effort.

But that's only one part of the whole and, although most of us would happily settle for that much, we have to turn the page to continue the story on the other side. The other side is, at first glance, more sombre. In the shadows the lines are softer, less bright; sometimes hard to see. Instead of the glow of colour, the darkness seems only to throw back a reflection of suffering. The arms held open in welcome become pale arms drawn tense on a cross. Rich reds dull into spilt blood. The song of joy becomes a groan of pain.

Yet it's still love. More splendid than the brilliance which dazzles me. It's just harder to recognise because it's not the way I'd paint it. Self-giving love; suffering, dying.

And if I'm going to share the splendour of love then I have to recognise the pain as part of it. Not just as a counterpoint, making the colour more brilliant in contrast with the dark, but as part of its reality.

In the recognition, understanding begins. When pain and disappointment hit me, I may still rebel and protest, but slowly, with infinite patience, God who is love incarnate leads me to see that love stands there in the shadows, just as he does in the light. Not necessarily creating the pain, but working through it with me for good – and slowly I am able to recognise some of the disguises of love. Slowly and hesitantly I begin to understand that his forms are myriad, and that love comes in ways I never thought possible. Love speaks not only in the still small voice, but also in the frightening storm, and in an infinity of guises. The adventure is to recognise him.

Lord, there are times
when silence seems best.

And yet, when I'm faced with your love,
even with the little I know,
I have to speak.
If nothing else, to say thank you.
I don't deserve it.
Now there's an understatement.
Sometimes all I am and do
seems designed to test your love to the limit.
And you go on loving.
Lord, it's breathtaking. Immense.
I hear your voice, carrying crystal clear over
*   the vast plain,*
reaffirming life and presence.
A small point of focus in infinity.
Infinity of love.
Great enough for all. Small enough for me.

A love that comes to identify, to tell me I
*   belong.*
That comes to strengthen, to tell me it's mine.
That comes to comfort with the knowledge
*   that you care.*
A love that comes to challenge and discipline
at the point of stress.
That stretches me nearly to breaking point
and makes me grow.
That faces me, in searching, insistent
*   strength,*

with the pain of truth I'd rather not see.
That strips my illusions and leaves me
    trembling, naked,
in the cold wind of honesty.
The love that fights me
as I struggle to preserve the lies I live
from the buffeting storm of your spirit.

And through it all,
a love that holds me, firm and close.
Making me aware, in the eye of the cyclone,
of your peace.
And in the wind-drop of understanding,
my ears still ringing, eyes still smarting,
    from the gale,
I recognise your love.
In the glacier wind as in the valley breeze.
Seeing, as in the crackling flash of brief
    lightning,
brilliant and clear,
some of the disguises of your love.

Lord, I know there's more,
but I'm not ready for it yet.

Taken from *Disguises of Love: Meditations and prayers* by Eddie
Askew, published by The Leprosy Mission. Used with permission.
Eddie Askew books can be purchased from www.tlmtrading.com.

Milton Keynes UK
Ingram Content Group UK Ltd.
UKHW020616300823
427742UK00010B/275